SUNDAY WORSHIP

God's Unchanging Order

AUGUSTIN D. ETIENNE

The Reading Glass
BOOKS

The Reading Glass
BOOKS

Contents

It has become necessary to lay out a case for Sunday Worship. This is so, not because God's Word needs defending, for it is more than able to defend itself. But it would seem that many are "willingly ignorant" of all that God has declared in His Word and consequently go about seeking to restate that which God has clearly declared in a way, which subtlely present God as less than omnipotent or omniscient. To present God in the light of a Saturday keeper is to present Him with hang-ups and limitations and in the valley of indecision. God, having said all that He has in the way that He has, would be having a mental lapse to have both systems running in the same place at the same time.

But God is a God of principle and standards. God says of Himself in Malachi 3:6 that as God He does not change. Many may argue that over time God changes in methods and manner but He really doesn't. When the panorama of man's history is considered as a whole the apparent becomes obvious. The God who declares that He knows the end from the beginning was consistent all along (Isaiah 46:9, 10).

Having established His consistency, God is now duty bound to perform. That which He requires of us today had been scheduled into His plan of activity from the onset.

CHAPTER 1

FALSEHOODS REGARDING THE USE OF SUNDAY

Papal Worship:

To worship on Sunday is to worship the Pope. That proposition is so untrue. The whole idea stems from the presupposition that Constantine, the Emperor of Rome, changed the day and that to subscribe to the Sunday is to revere the pope.

Of course Christians do not have the same regard for the pope as do Roman Catholics. One who is honest and truthful will readily admit that. So to say that Sunday worshipers worship the pope, whether knowingly or unknowingly, is false.

The other aspects of the falsehood that Constantine changed the day will be dealt with in detail as we treat the subject.

The Mark of the Beast:

It is also commonly said by Sabbath keepers that Sunday worship is having the mark of the beast.

Anyone who has read the book of Revelation 13:16-18 with any measure of understanding would have realized that there are several characteristics regarding the mark of the beast that make it impossible to be carrying the mark of the beast today.

For one thing, the mark of the best is a mark – a distinguishing mark, a visible mark, a mark worn on the body (either in the right hand or on the forehead). The location of the mark seems to suggest that the mark will be so prominent that it would be nigh impossible to conceal. Sunday is not something that could be worn. It is not something that only "those who carry the mark of the best have and use". It is a day; a period of time used both by Sabbath keepers and non-Sabbath keepers. Besides even the Sabbath keepers have Sunday night worship service. I can hear them sneering and conjecturing that the evening and the morning constitutes the day, thus their Sunday night worship is not really papal worship. But let me contend. If that is part of the effect of the declaration made by Constantine and that that is kept by Sunday worshippers, it would stand to reason that so as not to give the semblance of worshipping on Sunday that period of time would be carefully and conscientiously avoided.

Then, too, since Constantine legislated that Sunday would not be a normal working day, that Sabbath keepers in protest would open their business places and proceed to commence the week's activities on that day. But contrary to my supposition those use both the Saturday and the Sunday away from normal work.

A third reason why it is a fallacy to consider Sunday worship as carrying the mark of the beast is because the scripture makes it abundantly clear that any one who does not have the mark can neither buy nor sell during its existence. To say that the mark is Sunday is to say that the mark is in existence from creation or became such since Constantine passed his law. To say that the mark is in existence now is to say that the Anti Christ is even now reigning.

There are several problems with this line of thinking. The Bible tells us that the Antichrist will reign for over seven years (probably less than twelve). (That period of time is understood when we consider that he is going to confirm a covenant with the Jews for seven years. I suppose that given the Jewish attitude towards the rest of the world the anti-Christ will have to be someone that they had come to know and trust.) It has been decades now since Christians have been worshipping on Sunday and accused of carrying the mark of the beast. What kind of seven years are we talking about? Is it seven years of years or is it seven of the years, as we know it? It must be normal years for the book of Revelation gives us a breakdown of that period in days (Rev. 11:2, 3; 13:5).

> But the court which is without the Temple leave out, and measure it not; for it is given unto the Gentiles: and the holy city shall they tread under foot **forty and two months.**

> And I will give power unto my two witnesses, and they shall prophesy **a thousand two hundred and three score days**, clothed in sackcloth.

> And there was given unto him a mouth speaking great things and blasphemies: and power was given unto him to continue **forty and two months**.

This period covers the second half of the seven-year period.

Then, too, there is no free enterprise during his reign. Everything is censored. No one can buy or sell except those who carry the mark. Sabbath keepers today carry on their weekly activities as per normal. There is no restriction on them because they do not have the mark of the beast. This should be a compelling reason against the thought that the mark is already issued.

The time of the Antichrist is limited. During his tenure he establishes a peace treaty with Israel for seven years. It is in the midst of that seven-year period that he breaks his covenant with the Jews, sets up the abomination which makes desolate and ushers in the time of the great tribulation – the time of Jacobs's trouble. Is there a time of peace in Israel where the people dwell in safety? Has any agreement been signed with Israel within the last decade that could be regarded as the treaty that God spoke about? What about the great persecution which will ensue as a result of the breach of contract? How then could that mark already be in existence and how can it be Sunday? If the mark is not yet in existence then there is something drastically wrong with the doctrinal beliefs and teaching of Sabbath keepers. Of course they are wrong on that count and on many more.

Worshipping the Sun god:

Another fallacy regarding the use of the day is that people who worship on Sunday worship the sun god. It can be readily established that indeed pagans worshipped the sun as god and that Sunday was dedicated to such worship. It can also be established that there was a pagan god worshipped for each of the seven days of the week. The god worshipped on Saturday or rather on the seventh day of the week was the god Saturn – one of the planets in our solar system. Were we to dabble a little in logics one might very well arrive at the following conclusions:

Since all sun god worshippers worship on Sunday
Christians worship on Sunday
Therefore Christians are sun god worshippers.

Most assuredly then the following should also be true:

Since all Saturn worshippers worship on Saturday
Sabbath worshippers worship on Saturday
Therefore Sabbath keepers are Saturn worshippers.

That makes the Sabbath keepers idol worshippers. I am sure that the idea will be spurned as Sabbath keepers rationalize and seek to establish their adherence to their day on very different premises. Could the same privileges and leeway be allowed for those who worship on Sunday? Indeed they are the ones who have the greatest claims to the right day to worship. Yes, there is a right day of worship just as there is a right day of rest.

CHAPTER 2

THE COVENANT

It is an inescapable fact that there are several covenants given to God's people. That we see because of the varying terms and conditions given as God made those covenants. But we would, in this document, seek to limit ourselves to two and possibly three of these covenants.

The New Covenant:

One of the covenants we will concern ourselves with is the "New Covenant". Jesus Christ declared at the last supper that this is the "New Covenant" in his blood (Lk. 22:20; Mt. 26:28; Mk 14:24).

> *Likewise also the cup after supper, saying, 'This cup is the* ***new testament*** *in my blood, which is shed for you.'* ***(Luke 22:20)***

> *For this is my blood of the* ***new testament,*** *which is shed for many for the remission of sins.* ***(Matt. 26:28)***

> *And He said unto them, 'This is my blood of the* ***new testament****, which is shed for many.'* ***(Mk. 14:24)***

One verse in Hebrews 8 puts the whole covenant issue in the focus that we need here. In Hebrews 8:13, the Holy Spirit inspired scriptures inform us that by virtue of the fact that God says "A New Covenant…" He hath made the first old.

That is a condition that most of us would not readily have conjured and most definitely one that many are not prepared to accept. The first covenant is old and done away with. That is not my conjecture; it is the word of the Holy Spirit of God. *"Now that which decayeth and waxeth old is ready to vanish away"* (8:13). These indeed are hard words to be used in connection with that which God had established. But God used them. It is with great significance that He has used those words. It was He who reminded us that you do not put new wine into old bottles. Neither do you put a new patch on an old garment (Mt. 9:16, 17; Mk. 2:21, 22; Lk 5:36, 38). To attempt such a feat is to suffer loss. In the case of the garment, the 'rend' is made worse. In the case of the wine there is a total loss of both the wine and the skin. Judaism – law keeping – and Christianity cannot co exist.

No man putteth a piece of new cloth unto an old garment, for that which is put in to fill it up taketh from the garment, and the rent is made worse. Neither do men put new wine into old bottles: else the bottles break, and the wine runneth out, and the bottlers perish: but they put new wine into new bottles, and both are preserved. **(Matt. 9:16, 17)**

No man also seweth a piece of new cloth on an old garment: else the new piece that filled it up taketh away from the old, and the rent is made worse. And no man putteth new wine into old bottles: else the new wine doth burst the bottles; and the wine is spilled, and the bottles will be marred: but new wine must be put into new bottles. **(Mk. 2:21, 22).**

…No man putteth a piece of a new garment upon an old: if otherwise, both the new maketh a rent, and the piece that was taken out of the new agreeth not with the old. And no man putteth new wine into old bottles: else the

new wine will burst the bottles, and be spilled, and the bottles shall perish. But new wine must be put into new bottles: and both are preserved. (Lk. 5:36 – 38).

The Old Covenant:

What is the "Old Covenant" which is being replaced? The Old Covenant being replaced is the law given at Mount Sinai – Exo. 20:1 – 23:8; Gal. 4:21ff.

We go to Exodus 19:5, 6 to see what the covenant is. Many would consider just Ex. 20:1 – 23:17 the covenant that God made with Israel. No! It encompasses more than that. As a matter of fact the covenant is laid out in Exo. 19:5, 6.

*Now therefore, **if** ye will obey my voice indeed, and keep my covenant, **then** ye shall be a peculiar treasure unto me above all people: for all the earth is mine: And ye shall be unto me a kingdom of priests, and an holy nation…(Ex. 19:5, 6)*

This covenant is what we call a conditional covenant. The actions of God depended on the actions of His people. That is a two-way street; i.e. a give and take.

Two words characterize conditional covenants that God makes with His people i.e. "if" and "then". What God does depended totally on what the children of Israel did. *"If you will obey my voice indeed and keep my covenant…"* That was the responsibility of the Israelites. Their conformity to the words of God dictated God's response; i.e. *"then ye shall be a peculiar treasure unto me above all people: for all the earth is mine: and ye shall be unto me a kingdom of priests, and an holy nation."* God was obligated only as far as the compliance of the Israelites to His words.

Those words Moses communicated to the children of Israel to which they said 'No problem'! (19:8). They accepted the covenant and promised to adhere to all its dictates. God proceeded to lay out the terms and conditions of the **"words"** He wanted them to **"obey" and "keep"**. From chapter 20:1 – 23:17, God detailed His word to them.

From the offset there were signs of problems between God and Israel. There was no cordiality between them. The sound of His voice struck terror into their hearts. They could not stand it for any extended period of time. They plead with Moses to be a mediator between them and God.

God proved Himself to His people that day. He was real; He was present; He was powerful; He spoke with them. His presence had been with them in the pillar of cloud by day and the pillar of fire by night. Now they had heard Him; audibly, personally. He must have had a deep masculine voice. It sounded like thunder. It exuded power.

All that God required of them was recorded in a book. That book was then consecrated together with the people by the blood of a bull, part of which was sprinkled on the people and part on the book (Ex. 24:1-8). That blood made the covenant legal and binding. Subsequently, that book was referred to as the "book of the law" or simply "the law". When later reference was made to the law it was to the book as a unit and not to fragments of the whole. He who breaks one portion is guilty of all.

And he said unto Moses, 'Come up unto the LORD, thou and Aaron, Nadab, and Abihu, and seventy of the elders of Israel; and worship ye afar off.

And Moses alone shall come near the LORD: but they shall not come nigh; neither shall the people go up with him.'

And Moses came and told the people all the words of the LORD, and all the judgments: and all the people answered with one voice, and said, 'All the words which the LORD hath said will we do.'

And Moses wrote all the words of the LORD, and rose up early in the morning, and builded an altar under the hill, and twelve pillars, according to the twelve tribes of Israel.

And he sent young men of the children of Israel, which offered burnt-offerings, and sacrificed peace-offerings of oxen unto the LORD.

And Moses took half of the blood, and put it in basons; and half of the blood he sprinkled on the altar.

And he took the book of the covenant, and read in the audience of the people: and they said 'All that the LORD hath said will we do, and be obedient'.

And Moses took the blood and sprinkled it on the people, and said, 'Behold the blood of the covenant, which the LORD hath made with you concerning all these words'. (Ex 24:1 – 8)

God was very specific in the covenant that He made with Israel as being with them and not any other who would adhere to the terms and conditions of the Law. He said to them in Exo. 20:2 *I am the Lord your God; I brought you out of the land of Egypt, I brought you out of the house of bondage.* That was very specific. God had not carried out that feat for all and sundry – just for the children of Israel. It was because of this that God sought their allegiance.

Along with everything else, God gave them the Sabbaths – Ex. 31:13. It is strange that God uses the word Sabbaths – a plural. There was more than one Sabbath. Not only is the word Sabbaths plural, thus very interesting, but the subsequent pronoun referring to the Sabbaths is singular. The Sabbaths combined is a sign between God and Israel forever.

Again Moses singles out the Children of Israel as the other party to the covenant to the point of excluding ancestors – Deut. 5:2,3.

> *The LORD our God made a covenant with us in Horeb. The LORD made not this covenant with our fathers, but with us, even us who are all of us here alive this day.*

Moses reiterates the words of the 'book' to the people as he reminds them that they, and none else, were the other party to the covenant with God.

In Ex. 31:14 there is a phrase that is used and repeated several times in Leviticus eleven especially with regards to eating which is very significant at this juncture. That phrase is "**unto you**" or "**to you**". God was particular in making his covenant. It was with Israel and that He made abundantly clear (Ex. 19:5, 6). They were to be a peculiar people to Him. He repeats the fact that it is a covenant again in Ex. 31:17 but specifies that it is between Himself and Israel lest any other would think to lay "claims" or "rights" to the terms and conditions of the covenant

Many have realized the restrictive nature of the covenant and have sought to replace Israel with the concept of Spiritual Jews. That is impossible. God has since moved on and established a new covenant and has also negated many of the conditions that would have precluded us from the commonwealth of God (Eph. 2:11-22; Gal 3:1-29). God declares in His word that we are acceptable to Him when we are "in Christ" (Rom. 5:1, 2; 8:1-4).

> *Therefore being justified by faith we have peace with God through our Lord Jesus Christ: By whom also we have access by faith into this grace wherein we stand, and rejoice in hope of the glory of God.* ***(Rom. 5:1, 2)***

> *There is therefore now no condemnation to them which are in Christ Jesus, who walk not after the flesh but after the spirit.*

> *For the law of the Spirit of life in Christ Jesus hath made me free from the law of sin and death.*
>
> *For what the law could not do, in that it was weak through the flesh, God sending His own Son in the likeness of sinful flesh, and for sin, condemned sin in the flesh:*
> *That the righteousness of the law might be fulfilled in us, who walk not after the flesh, but after the Spirit.* **(Rom. 8:1 – 4).**

Our salvation and every other relationship that we share with Him are made possible in and through Christ (Eph. 1).

It is not our objective here to go into all of the ramifications of the book of Romans but suffice it to say that this book expounds our liberation and frees us to serve God in Spirit and in truth without the encumbrances of keeping the law (Ten Commandments included).

Having recognized the "Old Covenant" as being that given to Israel through Moses at Mount Sinai, we need to acknowledge the "New Covenant". The New Covenant in capsule is Jesus Christ. He is the initiator of the new covenant.

> *For if the first had been faultless, then should no place have been sought for the second. For finding fault with them, He saith, Behold the days come, saith the Lord, when I will make a new covenant with the house of Israel and with the house of Jacob.* **(Heb. 8:7, 8)**

He is the fulfillment of the New Covenant

> *In burnt offerings and sacrifices for sin thou hast had no pleasure*

> *Then said he, Lo I come to do thy will, O God. He taketh away the first that He may establish the second.* **(Heb. 10:6, 9).**

*But now hath He obtained a more excellent ministry, by how much also He is the mediator of a better covenant, which was established upon better promises. (**Heb. 8:6**)*

*For Christ is the end of the law for righteousness to every one that believeth. (**Rom. 10:4**).*

He is our hope of eternal salvation.

We shall see Him, as He is

*Beloved, now are we the sons of God, and it doth not yet appear what we shall be, but we know that, when He shall appear, we shall be like him, for we shall see him as he is. And every man that hath this hope in him purifieth himself, even as he is pure. (**I Jn. 3:2, 3**).*

The Bible tells us in Rom. 8:3 that it was impossible to be justified by the law because of the weakness of the flesh. The flesh was the major problem here. It was not subject to the law of God neither could it be (Rom. 8:7). But for those who are in Christ He says, we are now the Children of God (I Jn. 3:2). He refers to us as heirs of God and joint heirs with Christ (Rom. 8:17).

As children of God our relationship to him is different to that of others. Those who are not children are "none of His" (Rom. 8:9). But possessing the Spirit of God gives us all privileges and rights. Galatians chapter four confirms the relationship of the believer. As with an under-aged child, the servant had authority over the heir. The law was that servant who exercised authority even though the heir had 'potential'. As the heir comes to the age of maturity the servant no longer has authority over him but assumes the full role of servant even to the one over whom he once ruled.

Earlier we recognized that the flesh was the problem. Because of this problem of insubordination, God sent His Son in the likeness of sinful flesh and for sin, condemned sin in the flesh (Rom. 8:3). Now that sin and the flesh have been dealt with in Christ our new relationship is established through faith in all that Christ has accomplished. He has become our righteousness (Rom. 10:4). We no longer have to go about seeking to establish righteousness by keeping law – that question has been settled.

These few references quoted here in no way come close to summing up the new covenant but only serve to alert us that there is another covenant. Hebrews chapters 7, 8 tell us some more about the characteristics of the new covenant and the roles that it plays in the life of the believer. One of the more obvious aspects of those passages is that the first covenant had to be done away with in order to establish a second. In order to establish a second, the first had to be annulled (Heb. 7:18, 19). Even for Christ to become priest – our High Priest – the law had to be changed for the Mosaic Law made no provisions for priests from Christ's human tribe.

> *If therefore perfection were by the Levitical priesthood, (for under it the people received the law,) what further need was there that another priest should rise after the order of Melchisedec, and not after the order of Aaron? For the priesthood being changed, there is made of necessity a change also of the law....For there is verily a disannulling of the commandment going before for the weakness and unprofitableness thereof. For the law made nothing perfect but the bringing in of a better hope did; by the which we draw nigh unto God.* **(Heb. 7:11, 12, 18, 19)**

Many inefficiencies of the law have been exposed. Had man mooted these concepts, they might have been disputed and possibly rejected. But coming from the Omniscient God Himself leaves no room for contention and debate. Whether you accept it or not is a matter for you but that does not change the reality of what God has said and done.

One other thing needs to be said about covenants. There was one other covenant deserving of mention here. That is the unconditional covenant made by God with Abraham.

> *Now the LORD had said unto Abram, Get thee out of thy country and from thy kindred, and from thy father's house, unto a land that I will shew thee: and **I will** make of thee a great nation, and **I will** bless thee, and make thy name great; and thou shalt be a blessing: and **I will** bless them that bless thee, and **(I will)** curse them that curseth thee: and in thee shall all families of the earth be blessed. **(Gen. 12:1-3). (Emphasis mine)***

God made promise to Abraham that all the families of the earth would be blessed through him. That promise made specific reference to the Lord Jesus Christ as the seed of Abraham, the mediator of the covenant:

> *Christ hath redeemed us from the curse of the law, being made a curse for us: for it is written, Cursed is every on that hangeth on a tree: that the blessing of Abraham might come on the Gentiles through Jesus Christ; that we might receive the promise of the Spirit through faith. Brethren, I speak after the manner of men; Though it be but a man's covenant, yet if it be confirmed, no man disannulleth, or addeth thereto. Now to Abraham and his seed were the promises made. He saith not, And to seeds, as of many; but as of one, And to thy seed, which is Christ. **(Gal. 3:13 - 16).***

To that covenant we all as Christians have access. The covenant of the law coming four hundred and thirty years after cannot disannul:

> *And this I say, that the covenant, that was confirmed before of God in Christ, the law, which was four hundred and*

thirty years after, cannot disannul, that it should make the promise of none effect. **(Gal. 3:17).**

The weakness of the law is further demonstrated as we notice that while another can abolish it, it, of itself, can replace none.

For there is verily a disannulling of the commandment going before for the weakness and unprofitableness thereof. (Heb. 7:18).

God's covenant with Abraham had two major factors that allowed it to outshine the Mosaic covenant.

Firstly, it was an unconditional covenant. It stood in stark contrast to the Mosaic covenant and many others like it. Whereas God punctuated the Mosaic covenant with 'if' and 'then' here He simply stated 'I will'. God left the onus of fulfillment on Himself - His willingness to perform that which He had declared and also His ability to accomplish that which He was committed to. Thus failure of all that He had promised could rest only with Him. He cannot fail for He is God.

Secondly, it was a universal covenant – one that continues throughout all generations. All families of the world would be blessed by it. It seemed that for a time the promise was constricted. That was so only because in God's providence His plans were not in full operation. But as we consider the propositions of Galatians 3:13-29 and that of Ephesians 2:12-22 we realize that all that had transpired was part of the whole program of God. The issuing of the Mosaic Law was not supposed to supercede nor to supplant the promise but was only a stopgap measure until and paving the way for the real thing. We have statements like:

"...the law, which was four hundred and thirty years after cannot disannul that it should make the promise of none effect" **(vs. 17).**

Also, in verse 19 we read,

*"Wherefore then serveth the law? It was **added** because of transgression, **till** the seed should come to whom the promise was made... "*

***Before faith came**, we were under the law, we were kept under the law, shut up unto the faith which should afterwards be revealed. Wherefore the law was our schoolmaster to bring us **unto Christ**, that we might be justified by faith. **But after that faith is come**, we are no longer under a schoolmaster. (**vs. 23 - 25**).*

Galatians 3:26-29 tell us that our relationship to the promise exists only in Christ.

"For ye are all the children of God by faith in Christ Jesus. For as many of you as have been baptized into Christ have put on Christ. There is neither Jew nor Greek, there is neither bond nor free, there is neither male nor female; for ye are all one in Christ Jesus. And if ye be Christ's, then are ye Abraham's seed, and heirs according to the promise."

Ephesians 2:12, 13 tell us what was and is now in our relationship with and to Christ.

In the passages cited above several words stand out. In verse 19 we have '**added**' and '**till**'. These are words that make the Mosaic covenant very transient. Its lifespan was limited by and in time. Then there are the words '**before faith**', '**unto Christ**', and '**after that faith is come**'. All these words give the impression that the law was temporary. There is no mistake that the Law was not intended to be perpetual.

Many would jump at the opportunity to ask now "are we free to live as we please?" Yes! And No! Yes we can; but with grave and serious consequences to any misdeeds. Yes, because:

...if the Son therefore hath made you free, you shall be free indeed (Jn. 8:36).

"As free and not using your liberty for a cloak of maliciousness, but as the servants of God." (I Pet.2:16).

"Stand fast therefore in the liberty wherewith Christ hath made us free and be not entangled again with the yoke of bondage (Gal. 5:1).

"For brethren, ye hath been called unto liberty; only use not liberty for an occasion to the flesh (Gal. 5:13).

"Wherefore, my brethren, ye also are become dead to the law by the body of Christ, that ye should be married to another, even to Him who is raised from the dead that we should bring forth fruit unto God" (Rom 7:4).

We could not be 'more free' from the Law than a dead man is from the laws of his native country. No law can prosecute a dead man.

Thirdly, the covenant was a promise to Abraham of Jesus Christ the sin bearer. That covenant was all about God's veracity. Though it tarried it could not fail. Though, to us, much time had elapsed, yet with God it was *"in the fullness of time"* (Gal. 4:4,5) God does not count time as we do and is always on time in everything.

God's word is sure and is just as trustworthy as God Himself. God's word is Himself. Therefore the promise made to Abraham was just as sure as God Himself.

We are left in no doubt as to the scope and extent of the promise as the Holy Spirit through Paul expounds this promise to us in Romans 4 and Galatians 3. Though given to Abraham, the forefather of Israel who received the law, the promise was so meticulously guarded that God was particular not to allow it to be confused with that which the sign of circumcision covered. All that circumcision represented was encompassed in the promise but the promise was not in any way restricted by it. It is for this selfsame reason that we as Gentiles do not have to be covered by the misconception that to be beneficiaries of God's grace we must become 'spiritual Jews'. For in Christ – the promised seed – *"there is neither Jew nor Greek, there is neither bound nor free, there is neither male nor female, for ye are all one in Christ Jesus. And if ye be Christ's then are ye Abraham's seed, and heirs according to the promise."*(Gal. 3:28, 29)

Let me in passing say that the 'first covenant' being a conditional covenant was made weak because it depended on man's fulfilling his role in order that it might stand. Since man failed to keep his end of the agreement there was effectively no agreement:

> *My people are destroyed for lack of knowledge: because thou hast rejected knowledge, I will also reject thee, that thou shalt be no priest to me: seeing thou hast forgotten the law of thy God, I will also forget thy children.* **(Hos. 4:6).**

God Himself bewailed the fact that Israel never kept the covenant made with Him. He declares as much in Jeremiah 31:31, 32.

> *Behold the days come, sayeth the LORD, that I will make a new covenant with the house of Israel, and with the house of Judah: Not according to the covenant that I made with their fathers in the day that I took them by the hand to bring them out of the land of Egypt: which my covenant they brake, although I was an husband unto them, saith the LORD:*

But in the same breath, He, being the loving and merciful God that He is, made promise of a 'new covenant' that He would make with Israel. This would be in vast contrast to the first one in that the major base of the covenant will be different. Not again will He say 'if' and 'then' as in Exodus 19 but He uses a straight "I will" (Jer. 31:33, 34). Being dependant only on God's capabilities, there is a more sure hope that this thing will come to pass. So sure is it that it is repeated again in Romans chapters 10, 11 and again in Hebrews 8:6-13.

> *But this shall be the covenant that I will make with the house of Israel: After those days, saith the LORD I will put my law in their inward parts, and write it in their hearts; and will be their God, and they shall be my people. And they shall teach no more every man his neighbor, and every man his brother, saying, know the LORD: for they shall all know me, from the least of them unto the greatest of them, saith the LORD: for I will forgive their iniquity, and I will remember their sin no more. (**Jer. 31:33, 34**).*

> *But now hath He obtained a more excellent ministry, by how much more also He is the mediator of a better covenant, which was established upon better promises. For if that first covenant had been faultless then should no place have been sought for the second. For finding fault with them, He saith, Behold the days come, saith the Lord, when I will make a new covenant with the house of Israel and with the house of Judah: not according to the covenant that I made with their fathers in the day when I took them out of the land of Egypt; becajuse they continued not in my covenant and I regarded them not, saith the Lord. (**Heb. 8:6 – 13**).*

CHAPTER 3

CHRIST'S RELATIONSHIP TO THE LAW

It is commonly contended that the Law cannot be abolished until it be fulfilled. Christ Himself made the statement that He had come to fulfill the Law and nothing of it – not one jot or one tittle – would pass away till all was fulfilled. It stands to reason, then, that since more than just "jot" and "tittle" of the Law has been done away with, it must have been fulfilled. Conversely, if the Law still stands today them most obviously its just demands have not been met.

One word of Jesus' statement stands out and is vital if we would traverse from Law to grace. That word puts a most volatile timer on the process that to ignore it is to run the risk of missing God's grace altogether. That word throws the development of the abolition into a time lapse that it would seem that many have not been even aware of its existence. For, to think that one would deliberately ignore such a powerful presence is to witness a case of spiritual suicide.

That one dynamic word used by Jesus in that oft quoted statement is the word "till". It is an abbreviation of the word until. Until is a preposition of time. That preposition of time is the link between anything that will pass from the Law and the time of its fulfillment.

By definition, Webster's Dictionary gives the meaning of until as: (1) up to the time of (a specific time or occurrence); (2) before (a specific time); (3) up to or towards. As a conjunction: (1) up to the time when or that (until you leave); (2) to the point, degree, or place that (cook until done); (3) before: used with a negative (not until he tells you).

Young's Analytical Concordance to the Bible says that in this particular reference the word is used to mean "up to". A comparable statement is found in Matthew 24:38. The people carried on until the day that Noe entered into the Ark. It suggests a point in time when a previously occupying practice is discontinued.

In the light of this revelation Christ was not saying that it was impossible for the Law to pass away. Neither was He saying that it will never pass away. He was simply saying that it would not pass away until its designated time. There was a time set for its accomplishment. Though that was soon, still it was not yet time.

Many have used this passage to affirm that the Law is still in existence today. To do that is to deny the work of Christ. Others reluctantly concede that Christ did fulfill the Law but partially. The ceremonial Law was satisfied, done away with but not the moral Law. This is why we no longer have to bring the blood of animals to atone for our sins.

Isn't it ironic to think that God would do away with the solution to a problem and not deal with the problem its self when it was within His power to do so and that was the very purpose for which He came? That what we are looking at is a seeming replacement for the Levitical sacrifices and not a solution to man's sin problem?

Let me propose to you that Christ did not simply remove what prefigured His death by replacing it but He indeed satisfied the just demands of the Law. The Law demanded that every transgressor die for each and every transgression. The wages of sin (singular) is death (Rom. 6:23). There was and still is none righteous – God's conclusion (Rom. 3:10). The Law made nothing perfect. The Law simply gave an awareness of sin (Rom. 3:20). Adherence to the Law cannot save for salvation is by grace through faith (Eph. 2:8, 9). The Law is not of faith (Gal 3:12) therefore it has no bearing on our Christianity today (Galatians 3:1-12). Our hope is in our total dependence on what Christ has done for us and not by works of righteousness which we have done or will do (Tit. 3:5).

Why do we not sin (i.e. Break the Law)? Romans chapters 5 and 6 make it abundantly clear that when we come into the new covenant – that new relationship with Christ – our lifestyle is affected. We are new persons, not the old ones driven by the cravings of the flesh.

God has accepted Christ's substitutionary death as full satisfaction for our sins (plural} present, past, potential. God says of Christ's work that it is the propitiation for our sins [Rom.3:2, I Jn. 2:2; 4:10]. He is the appeasement or conciliation for my sin; consequently, I am in favor with God. He is favorably disposed toward me; therefore, I am the beneficiary of His grace. The frightening thing to many is 'can He or would He change His predisposition towards me – one in Christ – to becoming my judge?' Romans 8:28 –39 anticipated your fears. Who can lay any charge against you? It is Christ, but He is the very one who justifies you. Your just or rightful accuser is your advocate or mediator.

God accepts Christ as adequate satisfaction to His just demands for the wages of sin. Christ fulfilled the Law. The obvious has come to the fore. Since Christ satisfies the Law's demands – fulfilled it – does the law still stand and have jurisdiction over us?

In attempting to answer this question, we must acknowledge some things. There are quibbles concerning which Law is abolished or satisfied? In doing this we must acknowledge that there were at least five sets of laws in the book of the Law. There were the Moral Law – 10 commandments; the Civil Law – relationship of the people to each other; the Ceremonial Law - for cleansings for sin and impurities; Laws for the Tabernacle; and Laws for the Priests. Let us consider these.

The Moral Law is that which establishes our legitimacy to a right relationship with God. Such a relationship establishes our righteousness before God. But alas – God looked down and saw that there is none righteous, no not one. He declared the same in Romans 3. No chance. Not one single person qualified under the provisions of the Moral Law. Of course we don't all break the same ones in the same way, but any violation, regardless of how simple or atrocious warrants the same condemnation. Many will readily acknowledge that if you will break one you are guilty of all. But of course that is for the next person! Is it possible for me to break any?

Before you answer, let me remind you that God says in 1 John 1:8, 10 *"If we say we have no sin we deceive ourselves and the truth is not in us. If we say that we have not sinned, we make Him a liar and His word is not in us".*

But let me hasten to say also that God's word allows for us to carry out self examinations and come to a human conclusion - I Jn. 3:19 – 21. Considering the fact that we don't have perfect knowledge we are allowed to work with what we know. If after self-examination our hearts or our conscience does not put a finger on anything amiss in our lives, we have confidence toward God. We can say, "as far as I know...."

And hereby we know that we are of the truth, and shall assure our hearts before Him. For if our hearts condemn us, God is greater than our heart, and knoweth all things. Beloved, if our hearts condemn us not, then have we confidence toward God. (I Jn.3:19 – 21)

Jesus Christ satisfied the Moral Laws fully, so much so that God declares in Romans 10:4 *"Christ is the end of the Law for righteousness to every one that believeth."* Here we have the question of the time in the "till" of Matthew 5:28 being fulfilled? Since Christ's provision was satisfactory the 'jots' and 'tittles' can go. They have been fulfilled.

The Civil Laws governed the relationship with each other and were the laws of the State. Christ paid His taxes. Even when He seemed to be cashless, He did not evade. He had Peter catch a fish and pay their taxes with money from the mouth of the fish.

One example of the change we speak about is in Matthew 5:38, 39 *"Ye have heard that it hath been said, 'An eye for an eye, and a tooth for a tooth:' But I say unto you, that ye resist not evil: but whosoever shall smite thee on thy right cheek, turn to him the other also.* "That comes from the Civil Laws of the people. Christ was, by virtue of the statements made in this chapter, superseding what had been given before thus making them obsolete.

Christ's attitude towards others was unparalleled. He was generous, philanthropic, sympathetic, and empathetic, you name it. He could not be more forgiving that He was as He hung there on the cross. He begged the Father's forgiveness on those who had so inhumanely, brutally and even at the time so callously ill treated Him. He was not deserving of the cruelty that He endured yet He was not bitter against His enemies.

Unforgiveness is one of the most prominent and devastating sins among people who call themselves children of God. We are crippled and jeopardised daily by the debilitating effects of this cancer. The most fearful thing about it is that it has the potential to reverse the effects of God's forgiveness upon our lives.

For if ye forgive men their trespasses, your heavenly Father will also forgive you: But if ye forgive not men their trespasses, neither will your Father forgive your trespasses. ***(Matt. 6:14, 15)***

*Then his lord, after that he had called him, said unto him, O thou wicked servant, I forgave thee all that debt, because thou desiredst me; shouldest not thou also have had compassion on thy fellowservant, even as I had pity on thee? And his lord was wroth, and delivered him to the tormentors, till he should pay all that was due unto him. So likewise shall my heavenly Father do also unto you, if ye from your hearts forgive not every one his brother that trespasses. (Matt. **18:32-35**).*

It is the most fearful thing for a Christian not to forgive. Often we wait for the next person to come to us and even then we condescendingly, reluctantly, grudgingly acquiesce. The opportunity to forgive should be a joy for us as a Christian for there are three very important reasons why we should forgive. For one thing, it is a healthy thing to do. It releases a person of much emotional stress. Many are sick because of grudges they carry. Secondly, it gives us an opportunity to claim God's forgiveness. He has promised that if we forgive others He will forgive us. If we do not forgive others, neither will he forgive us. Thirdly, it gives God a basis for forgiving us. God is gracious but in this instance He has laid down the principle that if we forgive, then he will forgive. Our act of forgiveness binds God to forgive us when we cry out to Him for mercy.

Christ is the supreme example of forgiveness. In demonstrating forgiveness, He displayed love. By His own admission, love fulfills all of the requirements of the law. That He manifested without reservation throughout His earthly life. Of course what greater love is there than that a man should lay down His life for His friends (Jn. 15:12-14)? But Christ demonstrated His love for us even when we were His enemies (Rom. 5:6-12).

Our demonstration of love for God and love for our fellowmen answers all the requirements of the Law. Jesus said to the Lawyer in Matthew 22:34-40 that on these two principles (commandments) hang all the Law and the Prophets. The Law and the Prophets of course is reference to the entire Old Testament. All the principles laid out in the Old Testament are encompassed in these two commandments.

The Ceremonial Law, the Laws for the Tabernacle and the Laws for the priests could not more easily be fulfilled. They of themselves were merely shadows of that which existed in heaven and were communicated to man. They are all part and parcel of the exact system that persists in Heaven.

To indulge in this exercise seems redundant for the book of Hebrews clearly spells out everything; but because of the prevalence of misinformation (for many will not read the Bible for themselves but accept what is said by others) and the growth of these falsehoods, it bears repeating the truths that are being subverted.

Allow me to follow the sequence of the Book of Hebrews from chapter seven through ten. Much is said here and it would be tedious to repeat all but let it suffice to pinpoint some of the relevant information that is deliberately misrepresented.

The word 'Law' as has been mentioned before, is used to refer to the book of the Law which contained all of the Law without distinguishing sections - compare Exodus 24:3-8 and Hebrews 9:15-23. As a compendium it is always referred to as a unit – the Law. It was that book Moses sprinkled with blood, thus sealing the covenant between Israel and God (Ex. 24:3-8 cf. Heb. 10:15-23).

In Hebrews chapter seven the Holy Spirit deals with the Laws for the Priests. The first thing dealt with was the order of priests. In the priesthood of Melchisedec there seemed to have been no ancestry nor was there a successor. The perpetuity of his order comes into sharp focus. It was unique. Next we see the superiority of that priestly order. Great men like Abraham paid tithes to that order. Even the Levites who were made priests under the Mosaic Law were subordinated to that priesthood in that their great grandfather Abraham paid tithes to that order and received a blessing though he had the promise (4-10). The lesser is blessed of the greater.

But the Levitical priesthood was inadequate. The priesthood, together with all that was communicated through them, was wanting (vs. 11). Consequently that priestly line was changed together with all that came with it. *The priesthood being changed, there is made of necessity a change also of the Law* (vs. 12).

Christ's priesthood was further exalted in that He did not come from a priestly line. Had He come from the tribe of Levi, He would simply have been perpetuating the Levitical priesthood. But the priesthood changed and so did the Law.

The Law went through such a drastic change that it was terminated. Many have asked whether the Law is abolished. I believe Hebrews seven puts the question beyond the shadow of a doubt in a very legal manner. I have deliberately left this argument until now instead of dealing with it in verse twelve because I can hear some say that God was only dealing with the laws governing the priesthood. But such a claim cannot be made here.

In Hebrews seven verses eighteen and nineteen, reference is made to the Law.

> *For there is verily a disannulling of the commandment going before for the weakness and unprofitableness thereof. For the law made nothing perfect, but the bringing in of a better hope did; by the which we draw nigh unto God.*

Here it cannot be argued that this was only the Ceremonial Law or the Law for the Priests. The Laws for the priest were never designed to make anything perfect. These simply governed the appointments, rules and regulations concerning priestly personnel. The Moral law was so designed. If the statements of these verses affect anything, it must be the entire chronicle of Law. What is said here is very powerful. The word "disannulled" here means to cancel, to break, to make void. We learn here that the Law was discontinued with the advent of that new order of priest and its concomitant regulations. The Bible tells us that the Law was given by Moses but grace and truth came by Jesus Christ (Ja. 1:17). Grace and the Law are not concordant in Christianity. Ephesians 2:8 tells us we are saved by grace though faith. But then the law is not of faith (Gal. 3:12). Therefore the dispensation of Law and that of grace are oceans apart - probably as far as the east is from the west.

Christ in His personality far outweighs anything that the Law could provide. As a matter of fact Christ goes above and beyond anything that could be gained from the law.

> *"For such an high priest became us, who is holy, harmless, undefiled, separate from sinners, and made higher than the heavens; who need not daily, as those High Priests, to offer up sacrifices first for his own sins, and then for the people's: for this He did once when He offered up Himself"* **(Heb. 7:26, 27).**

In chapter eight the author (I believe Paul) continues to delineate the superiority of the priesthood and the tabernacle within which this superior High Priest officiates. Several things come to light in this passage regarding the place of sacrifices.

Firstly, it is called the "true tabernacle." To call this one true is not to say that the other was false but the distinction is made to show that all that we had seen on earth was a mere shadow of the real thing. It is an ancient black and white photo of the colorful original. Secondly, the temple was not made with human hands. It is one that the Lord pitched. The language of course bears reference to what happed on earth. But God was very meticulous in directing Moses to follow precisely the pattern revealed to him on the mount. With all of the information that we have received it would seem that everything has come around full circle to the crux of the matter – the covenants. That was then, this is now. Then the Mosaic system with all the Laws was fair enough. But now (vs. 6) *"Christ has obtained a more excellent ministry…"* The ministry of Christ is to reconcile man to God.

*For He is our peace who hath made both one, and hath broken down the middle wall of partition between us; having abolished in his flesh the enmity, even the law of commandments contained in ordinances: for to make in himself of twain one new man, so making peace; and that He might reconcile both unto God in one body by the cross, having slain the enmity thereby: and came and preached peace to you which were afar off, and to them that were nigh. For through Him we both have access by one Spirit unto the Father. (**Eph. 2:14 – 18**)*

For it pleased the Father that in him should all fullness dwell: and, having made peace through the blood of His cross, by him to reconcile all things unto Himself; by Him, I say, whether they be things in earth, or things in heaven. And you, that were sometimes alienated and enemies in your mind by wicked works, yet now hath he reconciled in the body of His flesh through death, to present you holy and unblameable and unreproveable in His sight; if ye continue in the faith grounded and settled, and be not moved away from the hope of the gospel, which ye have heard, and which was preached to every creature which is under heaven; whereof I Paul am a minister: **(Col. 1:19-23).**

...and that He died for all, that they which live should not henceforth live unto themselves, but unto him which died for them, and rose again. Wherefore henceforth know we no man after the flesh: yea, though we have known Christ after the flesh, yet now henceforth know we Him no more. Therefore if any man be in Christ, he is a new creature: old things are passed away; behold, all things are become new. And all things are of God, who hath reconciled us to himself by Jesus Christ, and hath given to us the ministry of reconciliation; to wit, that God was in Christ, reconciling the world unto Himself, not imputing their trespasses unto them; and hath committed unto us the word of reconciliation. Now then we are ambassadors for Christ, as though God did beseech you by us: we pray you in Christ's stead, be ye reconciled to God. For He hath made Him to be sin for us, who knew no sin; that we might be made the righteousness of God in Him. **(II Cor. 5:15-21).**

The Law or old covenant could not reconcile us to God. As a matter of fact it alienated us from God; for by the law is the knowledge of sin. It only made one aware that one could not make it to God by one's own works.

Not only does Christ have a better Ministry, but also it is of a better covenant. The present agreement between God and men is said to be better. Better is the comparative of something good. Webster's Dictionary says 'better' means: (1) of a more excellent sort; surpassing another or others; (2) more suitable, more desirable, more favorable, and more profitable. The new covenant far surpasses the old covenant. That is not just obvious, it is stated.

But what of the promises? Those, too, excel. The better covenant is based on better promises – the conditions, the hope and aspirations. Now what sensible person would leave the better for the good when the only reason why they were compared and not contrasted is because the good had some value only in its time? It carried out its functions creditably. But now everything is better.

The ensuing verses (vs. 7 – 13) further exacerbate the disparity between the first covenant and the new. God gives promise of a further covenant that awaits the Jews as Jews. For them there awaits a total unparalleled restoration that could only come about because of the shed blood of Jesus Christ (Rom. 11:1-27). Every surviving Jew (the Remnant) will be saved (Mt. 24:13; Zech. 13:8, 9; Rom. 11:25-27).

How uniquely the first verse of Hebrews 9 ties in all the Laws. "The <u>first covenant</u> -<u>had</u>…"- possession not a state of being – i.e. was. What did the first covenant have? It had ordinances. It had a worldly sanctuary. Each of these was a vital section of the covenant but that was not all there was to it. The following verses delve into the operation of the tabernacle until we come to some critical stats concerning the tabernacle and its accompanying ceremonies. In verses 9 – 12 we see that all that pertained was temporary i.e. "for the time then present".

*"…which was a figure **for the time then present**, in which were offered both gifts and sacrifices, that could not make him that did the service perfect, as pertaining to the conscience; which stood only in meats and drinks, and divers washings, and carnal ordinances, **imposed** on them **until** the time of reformation. But Christ being come an high priest of good things to come, by a greater and more perfect tabernacle, not made with hands, that is to say, not of this building; neither by the blood of goats and calves, but by His own blood He*

*entered in once into the holy place, having obtained eternal redemption for us. (**Heb. 9:9 – 12**)*

The sacrifices, the gifts, eating of meats, drinks, divers washings, carnal ordinances – these were all temporary impositions. They were <u>imposed</u> on them <u>until</u> the times of the reformation. That reformation came with the advent of Christ who had everything superior. Christ fulfilled every requirement of the Law very admirably. In fulfilling the law, He accomplished all its demands. We no longer have to accomplish that which Christ has already fulfilled. The Law was a fore shadow of good things to come. Now that reality has arrived the shadow is irrelevant and insignificant. The cry of many at this juncture may well be – "can we now do as we please?" That question we will answer toward the end of this discourse.

CHAPTER 4

CHRIST AND THE LAW

"What was Christ's relationship to the Law?" is a question of much importance. Did Christ keep the law? Did He spurn it? Did He ignore it? Did He encourage adherence to it?

From all indications Christ kept the law while the Scribes and Pharisees did not. On numerous occasions we hear Christ calling them hypocrites and many unflattering names because of their dishonest behavior. On the outside they had the appearance of law aiding citizens but at heart, they were criminals (Mt. 15:1-20; 23:1-39)

In His admonition to the multitude and to His disciples Jesus required of them that they adhere to the Jewish principles but not to the practices of the Pharisees. His request suggested that He, too, followed the requirements of the Law; otherwise, He, like the Pharisees, would have been a hypocrite (Mt. 23:13).

But Christ's relationship to the Law was unique. Because of the purpose of His mission here on earth, Jesus Christ carried out a role. For Him, it was taking them from the known to the unknown. Jesus kept their Laws with them yet periodically breaking them in order to make a point. In Matthew 12:1-8 Christ's disciples broke the Sabbath Law. It was wrong to do any form of work on the Sabbath day. But in defence of His disciples Jesus referred the Pharisees to incidents that they were familiar with - David eating showbread; the Priests work every Sabbath Day. Their job required it!

Jesus Christ taught two very poignant lessons in His response to the Pharisees. He exposes their insensitivities as He berated them for their mercilessness. Though they seemed to be representing the cause of God, yet they did not do it with the sensitivities of God in their hearts. They were judgmental in their attitudes where God would have mercy.

Jesus Christ had a greater lesson to teach them though. To their protests He responded with reference to His pre-eminence.

The Temple was great. But there was a greater than the Temple in their midst and they had scant regard for Him. The greatest injury came as we consider the person for whom they had little or no respect. He was the Christ, the Lord of the Sabbath. He was not subservient to the Sabbath but had provided the Sabbath to facilitate man (Mt.12:1-8 cf. Mk. 2:27). The Sabbath was not instituted that man should be a slave to it – being particular that the Law was kept down to the letter of it.

Having said that, we must note at this time that never once did Christ or any one of the New Testament writers command or indicate that it was mandatory that Christians keep the Sabbath. Not once. Many have taken narrative passages like we have examined to suggest that the Sabbath was commanded for us. That is just not so. References are made to the Sabbath in the New Testament simply as historical incidents. In Matthew 5-7 – the Sermon on the Mount – Jesus Christ does display His superiority over the Law. He states repeatedly, "Ye hath heard that it hath been said…. but I say unto you…". The Old Testament requirements are being contrasted between what the Mosaic Law said and what Christ required.

Many have expressed dismay that every one of the other commandments is being kept while the Sabbath is rejected. Through no fault of ours; not once does the Spirit direct to make mention of "Remember the Sabbath day.." but every one of the other nine commandments is reinforced and repeated in the New Testament. In keeping with the new principles, which Christ established, the nine are fulfilled; but they are not fulfilled because Christians set out to keep nine out of ten. As a matter of fact there are many more than ten commandments for the Christian Church to keep (e.g. Eph. 4-6)

Christ definitely supersedes the Old Testament Law. We have seen in Hebrews 8 how He is the mediator of a better covenant based on better promises.

Not only did He supersede the law, but also He fulfilled the Law perfectly. In Hebrews 10:8, 9 Christ met all of God's demands for sin. The scriptures tell us then that He took away the first that He may establish the second. He took away that book of the Law, which stood against us. Christ is the end of the law to them that believe (Rom. 10:4).

Christ has redeemed us from the curse of the Law (Gal. 3:13). He took the condemnation for sin that we deserved that we should be set free. He justifies us who believe in Him (Rom. 3:24; Col. 1:13, 14; Tit. 2:14; Heb. 9:12; I Pet. 1:18, 19; Rev. 5:9).

"Christ is the end of the Law **for righteousness** (Rom.10:4). Righteousness is what allows us to stand before God. But we have none of our own (Rom. 3:10). We can only stand in the righteousness of Christ (Phil. 3:9; I Cor. 1:30). Not only is Christ our righteousness, but also He is our righteousness without the Law (Rom. 3:20-22). No Law is required to make us acceptable to God (Rom. 3:28). Sabbath keepers contend that adherence to the Sabbath is necessary for salvation. That is simply a lie (Rom.4: 13 cf. Gal. 3:17, 18). Keeping or not keeping a law cannot disannul a provision God has given to us by promise through Abraham. If that were the case, God would have been indebted to us, and our salvation would have been by works and not by grace (Rom. 4:2-5).

Christ died to the Law that we might virtually be dead to it.

Knowing that Christ being raised from the dead dieth no more: death hath no more dominion over Him. For in that He died, He died unto sin once: but in that He liveth, He liveth unto God. Likewise reckon ye also yourselves to be dead indeed unto sin, but alive unto God through Jesus Christ our Lord. Let not sin therefore reign in your mortal body, that ye should obey it in the lusts thereof. Neither yield ye your members as instruments of unrighteousness unto sin: but yield yourselves unto God, as those that are alive from the dead, and your members as instruments of righteousness unto God. For sin shall not have dominion over you: for __you are not under the law__, but under grace. (Rom. 6:9 – 14). (Emphasis mine)

Know ye not, brethren, (for I speak to them that know the law,) how that the law hath dominion over a man as long as he liveth? For the woman which hath an husband is bound by the law to her husband so long as he liveth; but if the husband be dead, she is loosed from the law of her husband. So then, if while her husband liveth she be married to another man, she shall be called an adulteress: but if her husband be dead, she is free from that law; so that she is no adulteress, though she be married to another man. Wherefore, my brethren, __ye also are become dead to the law__ by the body of Christ, that ye should be married to another, even to Him who is raised from the dead, that we should bring forth fruit unto God. (Rom. 7:1 – 4) (Emphasis mine)

We are in Christ and if we are in Christ we are new persons not subject to the previous laws that controlled us (Rom. 7:1-4). We are dead to the Law that we might be married to another who is Jesus Christ. The Law does not control us, so the Sabbath, which is included in the Law, has no jurisdiction over us. We have been made free (Gal. 5:1). We should remain in the freedom, which was procured on our behalf. Our responsibility now is to fulfill the "law of Christ" (Gal. 6:2). To return to the Law is retrogressive and not of God.

Christ is become of no effect unto you, whosoever of you are justified by the law; you are fallen from grace. This persuasion cometh not of Him that called you. (Gal. 5:4, 8).

CHAPTER 5

RELEVANCE OF CHRIST TO SUNDAY

The crux of the whole Sabbath day question is whether the day has been changed from Saturday to Sunday. Those who propose that it has been changed and wrongfully so are misled and of course when a blind leads the blind, they both fall into the ditch (Mt. 15:14)

Some things need to be said with regards to the Sabbath that would enlighten the eyes of the blind. The Sabbath Law was with regards to a rest day and not to a day of worship. If any one is guilty of changing the Sabbath it is those who use it as a day of worship. At the very onset God gave the Sabbath to the Children of Israel as a day of rest. They had not rested for some time while they were in bondage in Egypt under the forced labor by Pharaoh. God wanted to compensate for that and to establish a new pattern for the weekly cycle of the Jews. Of course God built on a principle that He had set Himself though there is no indication that it was ever used or commanded until now. Man had to work six days and rest the seventh. The Jews were now specifically required to do so.

What is most remarkable about the institution of the day among the Jews is that they were not even to go outside (Ex. 16:29). That is one of the first and most powerful restrictions placed on the observance of the Sabbath day. Today all Sabbath keepers are out of their homes contrary to the Sabbath law.

Another of the restrictions on the Sabbath Day was their gathering and preparation of food. This is a long chapter so we will pick out verses or passages to highlight.

Then said the LORD unto Moses, Behold, I will rain bread from heaven for you; and the people shall go out and gather a certain rate every day, that I may prove them, whether they will walk in my law, or no. And it shall come to pass that on the sixth day they shall prepare that which they bring in; and it shall be twice as much as they gather daily. **(Ex. 16:4, 5)**

This is the thing which the LORD hath commanded, Gather of it every man according to his eating, an omer for every man, according to the number of your persons; take ye every man for them which are in his tents. And the children of Israel did so, and gathered, some more, some less. And when they did mete it with an omer, he that gathered much had nothing over, and he that gathered little had no lack; they gathered every man according to his eating. And Moses said, Let no man leave of it till the morning. Notwithstanding they hearkened not unto Moses; but some of them left of it until the morning, and it bred worms, and stank: and Moses was wroth with them. **(Ex. 16:16 – 20)**

And he said unto them, This is that which the LORD hath said, **Tomorrow is the rest of the holy Sabbath unto the LORD***: bake that which ye will bake today, and seethe that ye will seethe; and that which remaineth over lay up for you to be kept until the morning. And they laid it up till the morning, as Moses bade: and it did not stink, neither was there any worm therein.*

And Moses said, Eat that today; for **today is a Sabbath unto the LORD***: today ye shall not find it in the field.*

*Six days ye shall gather it; but on **the seventh day, which is the Sabbath**, in it there shall be none. And it came to pass, that there went out some of the people on the seventh day for to gather, and they found none.*

*And the LORD said unto Moses, How long refuse ye to keep my commandments and my laws? See, for that the LORD hath given you the Sabbath, therefore he giveth you on the sixth day the bread of two days; abide ye every man in his place, let no man go out of his place on the seventh day. So the people rested on the seventh day. (**Ex. 16:23 – 30)***

Then there is the question of "Remember." Again our Sabbath keeping friends tell us the word "Remember" is placed at the beginning of the verse because of the tendency of man to forget. So as a reminder to us to keep it He said "remember." That is a lie. The commandments that they seek to uphold are already shattered. If you break one you are guilty of all (Ja. 2:10). The word 'remember' is placed at the beginning of that statement because God had given that commandment already. It was not being given as a first time command as were the others so God simply said 'remember'.

One other area of changing the Sabbath is with regards to traveling. No one in the house was supposed to work. Not the children, not the servants – male nor female, not the stranger, (some in the house keep it and some don't) not their cattle, not their ox, not their ass.... But wait! Why ox and ass? You see the ox was the farmer's tractor used to plough the soil. So the tractor was not supposed to work - not by the owner nor by any one else. The ass was the pick-up truck and also the Mercedes Bends. That took the family around. It was their transport. Having worked the week, it was to rest on the Sabbath day. Today those 'asses' (Mitsubishi and Toyota) work. Their owners travel great distances from their homes that they were not to leave, to keep the Sabbath. Now consider, who changed the Sabbath?

Let us come back to Christ and Sunday. There is great significance in recognizing Sunday as Christ meant for it to be recognized. Whether you call it Sunday or the first day of the week, or the day after the Sabbath, we mean the same day.

Christians have been falsely accused of keeping a day instituted by Constantine and imposed upon the Church. That could not be further from the truth. One of the things we must first recognize is that God does nothing haphazardly. The use of Sunday was a well thought out, well executed plan of God. Sunday was to assume great significance so God laid out activities that would bring it into sharp focus. The perpetuation of that day was something orchestrated by God Himself.

Sunday was a day set aside by God Himself for religious activity. In Leviticus 23:11, 15 and 16 we see God specifically marking out that day for specific activities that had direct relevance to New Testament practices that would follow after. Of course much of the Old Testament pre-figures or foreshadows what God would do through Christ. A careful study of the feast days seems to indicate that most celebrations were on a Sunday. Never was the Sabbath day used except where the feast was for a whole week or eight days, which would include a Sabbath day or two.

The first Sunday that Christ deliberately used for our benefit is the day of His resurrection. There are those who have tried to explain away the fact of Christ's resurrection on Sunday but cannot. The fact that Christ rose on Sunday has special significance to the believer and to the Church. Just as in the Old Testament God set aside the Day of the Lord as opposed to the Sabbath Day.

On the first day of the week, Sunday, the morrow after the Sabbath, Christ rose from the dead. That was preparation for introducing the day to the Church. Remember, the Church is the Bride of Christ and also the body that He is the head of. Much debate has arisen over how much time Christ spent in the tomb and on what day He actually died. Various ones hold different views as to the day He died, though most hold to a Friday death.

What is most important is not the day that He died but the day that He rose. What makes the Sunday resurrection significant is the fact that His death put an end to an old regime while His resurrection gave life to a new one. That new regime that Christ gave life to was that of grace through faith.

Christ had now made the way or entrance into the Holy of Holies possible since He broke down the separation that prevented entry (Mt. 27:51; Eph. 2:4; Heb. 10:19-25; 6:19). We now have access to God without the need for an earthly priest to mediate on our behalf. That is unique to the New Testament Church.

Then there is the very important factor of Christ being our wave offering to God. It would have been observed in Leviticus 23 that the wave offering was consecrated on the morrow after the Sabbath. It was the first sheaves of grain harvested by the Jews and brought to the Priest as an offering. It was not permissible for the priests to do the wave before God on the Sabbath day but was commanded that it be done on the morrow after the Sabbath. That was what Christ Himself would do. That was what Christ was.

For quite some time I had difficulty understanding the passage in John 20:17 where Jesus said to Mary, "Touch me not for I am not yet ascended to My Father". Not until I saw the connection between the significance of the first fruits/ wave offering and the fact that Jesus Christ is the first fruits of them that sleep (I Cor. 15:20, 23; Ja. 1:18), did I get what Christ had said to Mary.

That which was holy and an offering to the Most Holy Father was not to be defiled by the touch of unsanctified human hands before it was presented. Christ then had to have gone to heaven, into the temple not made with hands to wave that offering of His life before the Father, thus saying 'that is only the first, more to come'. What an awesome powerful accomplishment on our behalf. God, having accepted the 'first fruit of them that sleep' and knowing the quality of what He will later receive, was satisfied. Not only was Christ acceptable to God, but also we, in Him, are accepted before the Father.

That happened on a Sunday.

From that point onward, Christ utilized Sunday. Light has been made of the fact that Christians point to the fact that Christ appeared to His disciples on Sunday, but that does not take away from the significance of those appearances. Christ's resurrection was on Sunday. His first appearance to His disciples was on the same Sunday. Of noticeable importance, too, is the fact that eight days elapsed before Christ made His next appearance to them. He did not come the next day or the third or fourth day. Neither did he come the seventh day. He came back to them the next Sunday. This time Thomas was there. That says something about what Christ sought to establish.

Of great significance to this trend is Christ's next move for the Church. The Church was not to be another synagogue meeting where the law was discussed. It was to be a new entity since everything Christ was establishing was new. No new wine in old skins. The old Jewish practices were being done away with.

In keeping with the end of harvest feast that again typified what Christ was doing, Jesus deliberately commanded His disciples in Acts 1:4 not to leave Jerusalem until… They were to receive power to be witnesses and they would be witnesses in Jerusalem, Judea, Samaria and to the uttermost parts of the earth (Acts 1:8).

Jesus, until then, had been with the disciples for forty days (Acts 1:3). His request for them to remain in Jerusalem included another ten days, though they did not know that it would be that long. Why did Jesus wait until then to send the Holy Spirit? God waited 'til then because the Holy Spirit's advent had to fulfill the significance of the day of Pentecost. That was the end of the Old Testament harvest. And it was also the day after the seventh Sabbath – seven is a number denoting perfection. The work was complete. But God's celebrations are not on the day of rest. They are on a day when there can be much rejoicing.

That's what the Sunday is – a day of worship and much rejoicing. Saturday, I repeat, is not a day of rejoicing. It is a day of rest.

Christ set up the Sunday as a day of worship and there is much significance – even in the Old Testament – attached to the use of the day. Let no one by his false claims deprive or deceive you out of your day of worship. You are not under the Law.

CHAPTER 6

RELATIONSHIP OF THE EARLY
CHRISTIANS TO SUNDAY

It has been seen that Jesus Christ and none other introduced Sunday worship. That Jesus moved the disciples in that direction is evident. The Apostles did follow the teachings of their Lord. It was on the day of Pentecost that the Holy Spirit was given thus inaugurating the Church. It was on that day, the day after the seventh Sabbath, Sunday that Peter stood up and preached that famous sermon that brought about the conversion of over three thousand souls. From then on the Apostles used Sunday; they were not hard learners. One long crusade was started. They preached and taught and practiced their new religion daily and God added to the Church daily such as should be saved.

In Acts 2:46, 47 several things are noted in the practice of the Church contrary to that which was practiced on the Sabbath day. One of the first things we notice was the movement from a Sabbath day gathering to a daily gathering. Next we see that the purpose for the gathering was changed. Sabbath day meetings were to read the Old Testament Law and to discuss it. They did not have a New Testament like we have today. But with the new movement, the Church, the thrust of the discussions was Christ and His relevance to us. Reference to the Old Testament was made to tie up the loose ends of prophecy that had already been fulfilled before them that they did not seem to be aware of. Thus

Peter's message was offensive to the Jews and also that of Paul, as we will see later.

Another major change in the format of their meetings was in its purpose. It was for communion, fellowship and for worship. Then communion was daily. Maybe not with the same group all the time since they moved from house to house but it was in keeping with the command of Christ – "as often" (I Cor. 11:26). It is ludicrous the way some Sabbath keepers have made a crystal clear statement like this to mean 'once a year' and to change it from representing the death of Christ to representing a picture of the foreshadow of Christ's atonement for sin. They, in their myopia, are so focused on the picture that they have not realized that reality has come.

Fellowship among the early Christians was not a nominal thing. So intense was their fellowship that it was a great financial sacrifice to the local Christians. The resources of those who were from out of town or country were depleted and being a long way from home and having that strong desire not to miss the lecture sessions with the Apostles they became dependant on the local Christians. The locals did not consider it a bother but gave willingly and selflessly. But they had fellowship.

Then they had times of worship. They praised God. It was those praise sessions that piqued the curiosity of those who were added daily. They came to find out what was happening and soon were swept off their feet by the Holy Spirit. They stayed. They continued in the Apostles doctrine and in prayer and in breaking of bread. That doctrine did not originate with the Apostles but they just passed on what they had learned from Christ. The Holy Spirit was now reminding them of what Christ had taught (Jn. 14:26; 16: 7-14).

As the Church moved out of Jerusalem as Christ had asked them to – albeit because of persecutions - new challenges faced it. Of the new challenges the Church faced was no less a problem than its relationship to the Law. Paul seemed to have been at the center of that controversy since he was the major proponent of the Gospel (Rom 11:13; Gal. 4:16). To him was committed the task of evangelizing the Gentiles.

From the very first mention of his sermons in Acts 13 we realize that His message was the grace of God through faith in our Lord Jesus Christ. That did not include adherence to the Law and consequently not Sabbath keeping. But I hear many shout, 'Hey! He was in their Synagogue every Sabbath day'. Yes, He was at the beginning of his ministry in most cities that he went to. He went there because he was sure to get an audience there and the main point of discussion was the scriptures. Not everyone in a crowd is necessarily there for the same reason. Not so in a courtroom. Some are accused, some are accusers and still others are simply observers. There are also the lawmen and there is usually a magistrate or judge. The same is true at any public gathering. The fact that Paul chose to go there on that day does not indicate that he was there to keep the Sabbath (I Cor. 9:21; Gal 2:18; Acts 17:2, 3, 18-21). His preaching was most often controversial to the Jews and that is why we have Acts 15 and a book like Galatians in the New Testament.

It has often been said that the controversy was over circumcision but again those who propound that this is the case are presenting only a half-truth – a whole lie? In Acts 15:5 we find the agenda for the Jerusalem Council – the council that dealt with the problem. On the agenda was "circumcision" – that was given to Abraham; but there was also the "law of Moses" – law singular. Again no distinction is made with regards to any section of the Law. Instead it is contrasted to the grace of our Lord Jesus Christ. The Law was a system in total. Hence we have reference to it as a "school master" (Gal. 3:24, 25); a servant 4:1-5; as Hagar and her son vs.22 – 31.

It would serve us well to consider some of the passages concerning Paul's doctrinal teachings in the Synagogues on the Sabbath days. Some of these are most clearly seen in Acts chapters 17 and 18.

In Acts 17:2, 3, 7 we see the tenor of Paul's messages among the Jews.

> *Now when they had passed through Amphipolis and Apolonia, they came to Thessalonica, where was a ssynagogue of the Jews: and Paul,* ***as his manner was,*** *went in unto them, and three Sabbath days reasoned with them out of the scriptures, opening and alleging, that* ***Christ must needs have suffered, and risen again from the dead; and that this Jesus, whom I preach unto you, is Christ.*** *... Whom Jason hath received; and these all do contrary to the decrees of Caesar, saying that* ***there is another king, one Jesus.***

Here we are informed that firstly, it was his manner. That tells me that when Paul went into the Synagogues it was not service as usual. Things were different. Discussions must have been heated. It would seem that some tempers flared, as we will see later by the actions of those devout Jews. As Paul continued on successive Sabbath days it would seem that he dominated the discussions all the time. His message was centered on Jesus Christ, His suffering and death and resurrection. That was not the usual law school discussion. His discussions were not from their recent personal experiences with Christ but were from the Scriptures – Old Testament.

In verse 7 Paul is accused of teaching seditious doctrines. He is now presenting a Jesus Christ as King. That definitely was not church as usual. (Sounds like the crowd at Jesus' trial before Pilate.)

Paul went on to Berea and Thessalonica and had similar sessions there in their Synagogues. The people who heard accepted and believed the message of Paul until the jealous Jews came and created an uproar.

> *Therefore many of them believed; also of honorable women which were Greeks, and of men, not a few. But when the*

Jews of Thessalonica had knowledge that the word of God was preached of Paul at Berea, they came thither also, and stirred up the people. (vs. 12, 13)

Verse 17 says that he, Paul, disputed with them. It is obvious that they were not saying the same things. They were on opposite sides of the debate. In verse 18 other teachers got into the fray and castigated the teachings of Paul; yet they were curious enough to listen. They thought of him as a '*setter forth of strange gods: because he preached unto them Jesus, and the resurrection.*"

Therefore disputed he in the synagogue with the Jews, and with the devout persons, and in the market daily with them that met with him. Then certain philosophers of the Epicureans, and of the Stoicks, encountered him. And some said, What will this babbler say? Other some, He seemeth to be a setter forth of strange gods: because he preached unto them Jesus, and the resurrection. (vs. 17, 18)

From verse 18 to verse 34 we have a sample message from Paul. We hear the Athenians mocking and saying that he taught **"new doctrine"** or **"strange things"**.

And they took him, and brought him unto Areopagus, saying, May we know what this new doctrine, whereof thou speakest, is? For thou bringest certain strange things to our ears: we would know therefore what these things mean.

But he continued his apologetics till he showed them the relationship between what they were doing and what God required of them. No law there.

In chapter 18 the strain is continued of what Paul taught. In verse 5 he taught that Jesus was Christ.

And when Silas and Timotheus were come from Macedonia, Paul was pressed in the spirit, and testified to the Jews that Jesus was Christ.

In verse 11 he taught the word of God. We say this not to mean that the Old Testament is not the word of God but that distinction was being made between what used to be and what Paul was now doing.

And he continued there a year and six months, teaching the word of God.

In verses 12 and 13 it is stated very emphatically that Paul taught contrary to the law. That must have included discussions about the day of worship.

And when Gallio was the deputy of Achaia, the Jews made insurrection with one accord against Paul, and brought him to the judgment seat, saying this fellow persuadeth men to worship God contrary to the law.

In verse 28, Apollos, an eloquent orator, now convinces them publicly that Jesus is the Christ. He might not have minced words as he spoke to them and that publicly. He gave them no covering of the privacy of their synagogue to denounce their beliefs and false teachings but did it in a way that they could not come back with a logical defence after he had finished with them. The message of salvation was not a laughing matter, nor one open to neither speculations nor personal opinions.

And when he was disposed to pass into Achaia, the brethren wrote exhorting the disciples to receive him; who, when he was cone, helped them much which had believed through grace: for he mightily convinced the Jews, and that publicly, shewing by the scriptures that Jesus was Christ.

CHAPTER 7

THE POST-APOSTOLIC CHURCH FATHERS

Following the demise of the Apostles we had able men, well trained who were able to carry on the work of the Church. Some of them had been contemporaries of the Apostles and had worked alongside of them. The information that they handed down to other well able men was not watered down nor adulterated in any way but could have been verified by the last remaining Apostles and trained pastors like Timothy and Titus and others. Further, we had the Holy Spirit who has seen to it that the Scriptures that have come down to us were indeed that which was inspired by God.

One of the things those early Church Fathers passed on to their congregations was the day on which they met for worship. Several of these wrote years before the ascendance of Constantine to the Roman throne and indeed a long time before he was born. I want to quote extensively from the notes of the <u>Dake Annotated Reference Bible</u> to bring to our attention the fact that Sunday was the day recognized for worship by the early Church. Let me remind us that these notes are not inspired but are threads of historical evidence that are relatively easily verifiable. Some of those sources may not be commonplace in hard copies that could be purchased from any bookstore but with today's technology, they may be readily available on the Internet.

Dake – New Testament - Page 191.

Sunday the Christian Sabbath

The disciples of Moses teach that the Catholic Church changed the Sabbath from Saturday to Sunday by Constantine, 321 A.D., and by the Catholic Church, 364 A.D. The following facts from history prove that they are historically wrong.

1. The Encyclopedia Britannica under "Sabbath" and "Sunday" says, "In the early Christian Church JEWISH CHRISTIANS continued to keep the Sabbath, like other points of the law...On the other hand, Paul from the first days of GENTILE CHRISTIANITY, laid it down definitely that the Jewish Sabbath was not binding on Christians. Controversy with Judaizers led in process of time to direct condemnation of those who still kept the Jewish day...In 321 A.D. Constantine made the Christians Sabbath, Sunday, the rest day for the Roman Empire, but it was observed by Christians for nearly 300 years before it became a law by Constantine."

2. The New International Encyclopedia on "Sunday" says, "For some time after the foundation of the Christian Church the converts FROM JUDAISM still observed the Jewish Sabbath to a greater or lesser extent, at first, it would seem concurrently with the celebration of the first day, but before the end of the Apostolic period, Sunday, known as the Lord's Day, had thoroughly established itself as the special day to be sanctified (set apart) by rest from secular labor and by public worship. The hallowing of Sunday appears incontestably as a definite law in the Church by the beginning of the fourth century and the Emperor Constantine confirmed the custom by a law of the state."

3. The Catholic Encyclopedia on "Sunday" says, "Sunday was the first day of the week according to the Jewish method of reckoning, but for Christians it began to take the place of the Jewish Sabbath in Apostolic times as the day set apart for

public and solemn worship of God." This volume quotes a number of early Christian writings of the first, second, and third centuries to prove that Sunday was kept by Christians from the earliest times.

4. The International Standard Bible Encyclopedia on "The Lord's Day" says, "The Lord's Day in the New Testament occurs only in Revelation 1:10, but in post-apostolic literature we have the following references: the Epistle of Ignatius to the Magnesians, IX,1, 'No longer keeping the sabbath but living according to the Lord's day on which also our light arose... Acts 2:46 represents the special worship as DAILY, but this could not continue long. A choice of a special day must have become necessary, and this day would, of course, have been Sunday...Uncircumcised Gentiles, however, were free from any obligation of sabbath observance"...No observance of a special day of rest is contained among the "NECESSARY THINGS" of Acts 15:28, 29 ...A given day as a matter of divine obligation is denounced by Paul as forsaking Christ (Gal. 4:10), and sabbath-keeping is condemned explicitly in Col. 2:16. As a matter of individual devotion to be sure, a man might do as he pleased (Rom. 14:5, 6) but no general rule as necessary for salvation could be compatible with liberty wherewith Christ has made us free (Gal.2:1-21; 3:1-4; 5:1-4, 13).

5. We next quote from the ten volumes called, "The Anti-Nicene Fathers, "the writings of the early church fathers down to 325 A.D. and before Constantine and the Catholic Church are supposed to have changed the sabbath from Saturday to Sunday:

(1) Ignatius, Bishop of Antioch, who lived at the time of the Apostles, 30 – 107 A.D. He, like Polycarp, was a disciple of St. John and one who should know Christian practice among early Christians as to the sabbath, He wrote, "And after the observance

of the sabbath (that the Jews kept), let every friend of Christ keep the Lord's day as a festival, the resurrection day, the queen and chief of all days of the week… on which our life sprang up again, and victory over death was obtained in Christ… it is absurd to speak of Jesus Christ with the tongue, and to cherish in the mind a Judaism which has come to an end… If any man preach the Jewish Law unto you, listen not to him. For it is better to hearken to Christian doctrine from a man who is circumcised, than to a Judaism from one uncircumcised". (Vol1 pages63-82)

(2) In the Epistle of Barnabas, ascribed to Paul's companion by clement, Origen, and others, we read, "He says to them, "your new moons and your Sabbaths I cannot endure" (Isa. 1:13). Ye perceive how He speaks: Your present Sabbaths are not acceptable to me… I will make a beginning of the eighth day, that is, a beginning of another world, wherefore, also we keep the eighth day with joyfulness, the day on which Jesus rose again from the dead"

(3) Justin Martyr, a Gentile born near Jacob's well about 10 A.D. writes, "And on the day called Sunday, all who live in cities or in the country gather together to one place, and the memoirs of the Apostles or the writings of the prophets are read… But Sunday is the day on which we hold our common assembly, because it is the first day on which God, having wrought a change in the darkness and matter, made the world: and Jesus Christ our Saviour on the same day rose from the dead" (Vol. 1, Page 186).

In his dialogue with Typho, a Jew, Justin Martyr says, "Is there any other matter, my friend, in which we are blamed, than this, that we live not according to the Law, and are not circumcised in the flesh as your forefathers were, and do not observe the Sabbaths as you do? …Christians would observe the Law, if they did not know why it was instituted… For we too would observe the fleshly circumcision, and the Sabbaths, and in short all feasts, if we did not know for what reason they were enjoined you… How is it, Typho, that we would not observe those rites which do not harm us – I speak of fleshly circumcision, and Sabbaths and feasts? …The Gentiles, who have believed in Him, and who have repented of their sins...shall receive the inheritance along with the patriarchs...even although they neither keep the Sabbath, nor are circumcised, nor observe the feasts...Christ is useless to those who observe the Law... The Sabbath and sacrifices and offerings and feasts... have come to an end in Him who was born of a virgin... But if some, through weak-mindedness, wish to observe such institutions as were given to Moses...along with their hope in Christ...they shall probably be saved" (Vol. 1, Pages 199-218)

(4) Tertullian, presbyter of the North-African Church, who was born about 145 A.D. writes, "The Holy Spirit upbraids the Jews for their holydays, "Your Sabbaths, and new moons, and ceremonies my soul hateth... By us (Christians), to whom Sabbaths are strange... to the heathen each festive day occurs but once annually: you (Christians) have a festive day every eighth day... Others suppose that the sun is the god of the Christian, because it is a well-known fact that we pray towards the east, or because we make Sunday a day of festivity... you who reproach us with the sun and Sunday should consider your own proximity to us. We are not far off from your Saturn and your days of rest... It follows, accordingly, that, in so far as the abolition of carnal circumcision and of the Old Law is demonstrated as having been consummated at its specific times, so also the observance of the Sabbath is demonstrated to have been temporary". (Vol. III. Pages 70, 123, 155, 3114)

(5) In "The Teachings of the Twelve Apostles", written about 80 A.D. we read, "But every Lord's day (Sunday) do ye gather yourselves together, and break bread and give thanksgiving" (Vol. VII, Page 331).

(6) In the Constitutions of the Holy Apostles (2nd. Century) we read, Break your fast...the first day of the week, which is the Lord's day... after eight days let there be another feast observed with honour, the eighth day itself"(Vol. VII, Page 447)

(7) In "The Teachings of the Apostles," written 105 A.D., we read, "The apostles therefore appointed: ...on the first day of the week let there be service and reading of the Holy Scriptures, and the oblation (Lord's supper): because on the first day of the

week our Lord arose upon the world, and ascended to heaven" (Vol. VIII, page 668).

(8) Irenieus, 178 A.D. in arguing that the Jewish Sabbaths were signs and types and were not to be kept since the reality of which they were shadows had come, says, "The mystery of the Lord's resurrection may not be celebrated on any other day than the Lord's day and on this alone should we observe the breaking of the Paschal Feast…Pentecost fell on the first day of the week, and was therefore associated with the Lord's day."

(9) Clement of Alexandria, 174 A.D., says, "The old seventh day has become nothing more than a working day."

(10) Theophilus, pastor of Antioch, 162 A.D. says, "Both custom and reason challenge us that we should honour the Lord's day, seeing on that day it was that our Lord completed His resurrection from the dead."

(11) Origen, about 200 A.D. says, "John the Baptist was born to make ready a people for the Lord, a people for Him at the end of the covenant now grown old, which is the end of the Sabbath…It is one of the marks of a perfect Christian to keep the Lord's day."

(12) Victorianus, 300 A.D. says, "On the Lord's day we go forth to our bread and giving of thanks. Lest we should appear to observe any Sabbath with the Jews, which Christ Himself the Lord of the Sabbath in His body abolished" (Section 4, "On the Creation").

6. Eusebius, the Father of Church History, who made a history of the time between the birth of Christ and Constantine, and who lived 265-340 A.D. says, "From the beginning Christians assembled on the first day of the week, called by them the Lord's day, for the purpose of religious worship, to read the scriptures, to preach and to celebrate the Lord's Supper…the first day of the week on which the Saviour obtained the victory over death. Therefore, it has the pre-eminence, first in rank, and is more honourable than the Jewish Sabbath.

Were it not for the dishonesty of our hearts and minds, such quotations would not have been necessary. But because of the crooked and devious presentations of the Wicked One who, through some humankind, 'seeks to pervert the right ways of the Lord' it is necessary to lay again some of the early problems that the Church faced and still does face (Gal. 4:29). "As then… so it is now". Many who do not know their history are doomed to repeat the errors of the past. The devil has systematically obscured pertinent historical information and sought to highlight contentious items of the past that would only foster his cause. I fear, even as Paul, that for many, labour seems to have been in vain; but God knows the heart.

Most of the literature referred to today are not common. What people know of them is what the Sabbath keepers teach. Most people only have the Bible. Yet the present day Sabbath keepers are out bugling the message of the Babylonian corruption propagating their damnable heresies in the guise of teaching the truth of God's word. God forbid that the devil will have the last say; not in the presentation of His Holy Word. Much damage has been done, but even now may God snatch from the jaws of the lion those who are called by His name.

It must be noted, too, that with all of the criticisms being levelled at the historical church, up until the time that religious tolerance was permitted by Constantine, the Church adhered to the Word as the sole source of faith and worship. Leading up to that time the whole of the New Testament cannon had been recognized and widely accepted. It is only as the books became closed to the general public and became the private enclave of a selected few perverts that the message, not the Word, became obscured and people were plunged into darkness.

CHAPTER 8

EARLY CHURCH AND THE LAW

Many agree that the book of Galatians must have been written before the Jerusalem Council meeting of Acts 15. Paul might have heard of the problem escalating shortly after he had returned from his first Missionary journey and had addressed the problem immediately. Then, too, the problem might have been referred to the Jerusalem Council and then Paul wrote subsequently.

Whichever was the order we have the same outcome to the problem. The answer was a resounding "No way!" We need not keep the Law to be saved. You do not keep the Law in order to attain salvation neither do you keep the Law to maintain salvation. There are those who claim salvation by grace through faith yet must keep the Sabbath to be saved – unscriptural, devilish. "Not of works" yet you must work?

Let us begin in the book of Acts to establish the fact that the question before the Council was not simply circumcision but was indeed the whole Law. In Acts 15 from verse one the problem begins to unfold. The probe to the problem was the observance of circumcision. That was only the introduction. In the use of the word we have a figure of speech called a metonymy. That is the use of one word for another e.g. "the *soul* that sinneth it shall die" (Ezekiel 18:4, 20). "The same day, there were added unto them about three thousand *souls*" (Acts 2:41). The word '*soul*' in these verses refers to persons or people. It does not only refer to the one of the three parts of man.

We also have another closely related figure of speech used in Scripture that is sometimes utilized with the word circumcision. This figure of speech is called a synecdoche – "a figure of speech in which a part is used for a whole, an individual for a class, a material for a thing, or the reverse of any of these. (Webster's Dictionary Pg. 1444) e.g. "Man shall not live by bread alone…" (Matt. 4:4 i.e. 'bread' for 'food'). "Tell me, ye that desire to be under the Law, do ye not hear the Law?" Law here is not simply saying "ceremonial law" it is referring to the whole gamut of the Law. To restrict it to simply ceremonial law is literary dishonesty. "…they unto the *circumcision*" (Gal. 2.9) referring to the Jews as a nationality.

Having said that let us go back to Acts 15. What was happening in the book of Acts then, is the same thing we have happening now. There are those who would not deny the work of salvation by grace through faith but would quickly add 'you are missing something. You need to keep the Law.' Salvation of itself is complete in Christ and needs nothing to complement it nor to bolster it in any way. All that we do afterwards is not for salvation but as a result of salvation (Eph. 2:10)

That the problem was one of keeping the whole law is evident in vs. 5 and 24.

> *But there rose up certain of the sect of the Pharisees which believed, saying, That it was needful to circumcise them, and to command them to keep the law of Moses.*
>
> *For as much as we have heard, that certain which went out from us have troubled you with words, subverting your souls, saying, ye must be circumcised, and keep the law: to whom we gave no such commandment:*

It is clearly spelled out that the contention was one of keeping the law. Circumcision was the covenant sign. If you were willing to be circumcised, then you were bringing yourself under the rules and regulations of the whole Law. Circumcision was being added to grace by the Jews. But was that the plan of God? No!

The Apostles made it abundantly clear in this Chapter, in the book of Galatians and, indeed, to all the Churches that there was no synergism between the Law and grace

> *Therefore by the deeds of the law there shall no flesh be justified in his sight: for by the law is the knowledge of sin. But now the righteousness of God without the law is manifested, being witnessed by the law and the prophets; even the righteousness of God which is by faith of Jesus Christ unto all and upon all them that believe: for there is no difference: … Therefore we conclude that a man is justified by faith without the deeds of the law.* ***(Rom. 3:20 – 23; 28)***

> *Know ye not brethren, (for I speak to them that know the law,) how that the law hath dominion over a man as long as he liveth? For the woman which hath an husband is bound by the law to her husband so long as he liveth; but if the husband be dead, she is loosed from the law of her husband/ So then if, while her husband liveth, she be married to another; she shall be called an adulteress: but if her husband be dead, she is free from that law: so that she is no adulteress, though she be married to another man. Wherefore my brethren, ye also are become dead to the law by the body of Christ; that ye should be marred to another, even to him who is raised from the dead, that we should bring forth fruit unto God. (Rom. 7:1 – 4)*

> *For as many as are of the works of the law are under the curse; for it is written, Cursed is every one that continueth not in all things which are written in the book of the law to do them. (Gal. 3:10)*

> *For I testify again to every man that is circumcised, that*
> *he is a debtor to do the whole law. Christ is become of no*
> *effect unto you, whosoever of you are justified by the law;*
> *you are fallen from grace.* (Gal. 5:3, 4)

You are either totally under grace or totally under the Law. Woe to you who hold to the Law and only fulfil part.

Not only was the Sabbath question dealt with but the food question was also handled. The only food restriction placed on the New Testament Christians was 'meats offered to idols" and "things strangled" and "blood" (Acts 15:15, 27). Of course these restriction go back to what God had placed on the entire human race in Gen 9:4. That restriction is not only for Christians, but for the world.

> *But flesh with the life thereof, which is the blood thereof,*
> *shall ye not eat.*

To think that even today there are those who would seek to bring us into bondage to the very things that God has liberated us from is mind boggling. It flies in the face of God that He did not have it all together, but they have it - contrary to what God has allowed. Let us look in general terms at the arguments of Paul against Law to the Galatians.

Galatians 1:6 – The message that the Sabbath keepers bring is not Gospel; it is a perversion. In that perversion, genuine seekers are moved from satisfaction in Christ to what satisfies only the flesh. There is a measure of will worship (Col. 2:20-23).

Galatians 1:8, 9 – The message of Christianity will never change. If anyone comes with another message, even if it were an Angel, it is false. The dreams and visions of religious leaders of Organizations don't hold water when they are contrary to the expressed Word of God.

Galatians 2:16-21 – The works of the Law can never save you whether of itself or in conjunction with anything else. Most definitely it cannot work with grace – oil and water don't mix. Dead men don't respond to any legal requirements.

Galatians 3:1 – Law keepers are bewitched – to use witchcraft or magic on; cast a spell over. (2) To attract and delight irresistibly; enchant, fascinate, charm. It is obvious that this is the case as we consider the consuming zeal with which they endeavour to "please" God. "I will have mercy and not sacrifice," says God (Mt. 7:13; 12:7).

Galatians 3:2 - 9 – We did not receive the Holy Spirit by the deeds of the Law. The Holy Spirit does not need the Law to perfect His work. All that is necessary for the Spirit to function is faith. Believing that what He says He can and will do (Rom. 3:20, 21, 25, 28)

Gal. 3:12 – **The Law is not of faith**. To hold on to the Law is to demonstrate mistrust in God's ability.

Gal. 3:14 – The promise of the Spirit was given to us by faith. We have the Spirit of God dwelling in us if we are Christians.

Gal. 3:15ff – The Law cannot disannul the covenant of Promise that God made with Abraham of which we are a part by similar faith.

Gal. 3:19 – The Law was *added* for a time – *'till'*. The Law had a lifespan. It was added yes but only until Christ would come. It was never intended to be more durable. Christ has come. That has brought the tenure of the Law to an end.

Gal. 3:23-25 - The Law was **for the time** *before faith came*. Now that faith has come we are no longer under the law.

Gal. 3:24, 25 – The Law was a schoolmaster (tour guide) to take us to Christ. Now that we are in Christ, there is no need for the schoolmaster.

Gal. 3:26-29 – We are children of God as many as have put on Christ i.e. become Christians. Those who have been baptised into Christ – that is having identified publicly with His death, burial, and resurrection in our place for our sin are children. Having become children of God there is no ethnic, racial, demographic or denominational distinction among us. Let me hasten to contradict, yes clarify myself. We are not talking here of nominal Christians who are actually non-Christians. We refer to those who have been transformed as a result of the application of the shed blood of Christ to that life.

Note well that there are no "Jews" in Christianity. Even if one is of the Jewish race when one becomes a Christian, one is referred to as a Christian – nothing more, nothing less. So to call oneself a Spiritual Jew is definitely not a Christian terminology.

Gal. 4:1-7 – An heir goes through at least two phases in his lifetime. While a minor, under aged, his inheritance, though obvious, is under the control of another who also is in control of him. But there comes a time, whether based on his age or a date on the calendar, when that heir takes up the responsibility of managing his inheritance himself. He is no longer under tutelage neither is his inheritance in trust.

That was the situation with mankind (Christians). Before Christ came, man was under the Law. Now that Christ has come He paid a redemptive price to free man from the grip of the Law, and to make us sons of God by adoption. Even with this relationship we are majors with full responsibility for our actions.

Gal. 4:9-20 – What great disappointment! The very same things that the Galatians had been saved from, i.e. observing days and months and times and years – (weak and beggarly elements), were what they were being drawn back into. The hurtful thing about this is the passion with which the proponents propagate their falsehood – no different today. Paul was fearfully concerned about them. His fear was not like that of a parent watching a toddler go off balance, but one of dread, fearing the worst.

Gal. 4:21-28 – It bears repetition and expansion that we would understand the real significance of those events that we seem to know so well. For once, we have an allegory in the Scriptures; but the real significance is immediately made plain. That is not to say that the Scriptures are replete with such but this one time was identified. What does it mean?

Here we have two covenants being contrasted. Note well that one covenant is being represented by Mt. Sinai. What is most conspicuous here is that no dissection is made in the Laws received at Sinai. It is all 'the Law'. It is all referred to as bondage. Now in many places we, together with the immediate hearers, are being cautioned against returning to bondage (slavery – Rom. 8:15, 21; II Cor. 11:20; Gal. 2:4; 4:3, 9, 25; Heb. 2:15; II Pet. 2:19). That is neo-enslavement by our peers cf. Gal. 5:8. But we are of the Jerusalem from above – free. We, like Isaac, are the children of promise (vs. 28).

Gal. 4:29 – The early Christians were persecuted for their simple faith in Christ plus nothing. Ishmael persecuted Isaac. The 'spiritual Jews' persecuted the early Christians and it is no different today. Sabbath keepers persecute Christians with regard to the Law. "As then…so it is now".

Gal. 4:30 – "Nevertheless" – Despite the fact that the situation is what it is, here is the solution to the problem. **Cast out the bondwoman and her son.** That is the Sinai covenant and Ishmael. How much more plain can the scripture be regarding the relationship between Christian freedom and adherence to the Law? "…throw out the bond woman and her son," they cannot be heirs together with the free. **"We are not children of the bondwoman,"** (vs. 31).

Gal. 5:1 – 8 - Here Paul bellows the clarion call to Christians while he sounds the death knell to legalists. It is obvious that it would be futile to require circumcision of Christians today when the Scripture is so clearly against it. Because of that the devil has shrouded the catastrophic cannon of rebellion against God in the form of seeming compliance to God's word. Man is required to keep the fourth commandment in seeming deference to God. But what this in fact accomplishes is to establish a system of works for salvation, instead of faith which God accepts. Many ignorantly follow that path of destruction as they look up at misplaced hope of eternal salvation.

I was appalled as I listened to a taped radio call-in program where one Osmond Baptist of Florida told a lady in Trinidad that even if she had accepted Christ as her personal saviour, because she did not keep 'the day' she was not saved. To support his claim he used the passage in Matthew 15:9 "In vain do they worship me teaching for doctrine the commandment of men". His claim was that her worship was in vain since she worshipped on Sunday and not on the Sabbath day – Saturday. How ridiculous and unscriptural.

First, the verse was taken totally out of context to make it refer to something Constantine, emperor of Rome had said and then back again to Christ and what he meant. Jesus Christ was here talking to the Pharisees and what they had done with God's Law and in forcing others to comply. They had twisted all that God had commanded to what suited their whims and fancies while they did not adhere to their maxims.

Secondly, nowhere else is that concept supported by Scripture. On the contrary, there are lots of verses that speak against those who would bring man again to such bondage. Romans 14:1-6 is one such passage. I Timothy 4:1-5 forewarns of such demonic developments. I believe that those who do not hold on to the Law have been too condescending and tolerant of those damnable views while the proponents of these falsehoods have been very offensive in seeking to take away the very hope that Christ came to give. I say too tolerant not in terms of violence but in allowing such heresies to flourish unchallenged. Too often heresies are allowed to spin out of control before they are redressed. Consequently Christianity has left the impression that there are no definitive doctrines but rather everything is in flux. Jude encouraged us to "earnestly contend for the faith". Today, as then, there are those who would subvert the truth to their own ends. If not exposed early, they blossom into seemingly plausible alternatives or adjuncts to Christianity. The early Church did not accept those changes regardless of how subtle and appealing they might have appeared. The truth does make a difference.

CHAPTER 9

NEW TESTAMENT TEACHING ON CRITICISMS OF THE SUNDAY WORSHIPPERS

In our foregoing discourse we have been apologetic concerning worshipping on Sunday, hopefully to the chagrin of our opponents. We have established the fact that Sunday holds special significance in the worship and life of the Church. We have recognized that the day was not established by the Apostles nor by Constantine as purported but by Jesus Christ Himself by a series of activities both sequential and commemorative in nature. Worship on Sunday clearly differentiates Christianity from a simple continuance of Judaism and from a transfer of Old Testament legalism to a refreshing New Testament liberty. We have neither doubts nor fears that this is what God intended and initiated.

Not only does God positively identify Himself with the recognition of Sunday, He further prohibits the criticism of those who worship on that day. In Romans 14:4-6 we have a very interesting situation that requires a brief observation. God is specifically saying to Sabbath keepers, 'you are out of line'. That is a simple and nice way to express what God has said to them. God is amazing. Here He asks some pertinent questions and makes very terse statements which should have forestalled this discussion. But that was not so and maybe not to be. Sabbath keepers have no regard for this part of the Word of God. Again they make themselves offenders of the laws of God. What does God require?

Quite frankly, God says in this passage – "that is not your business whether one maintains ones standing of righteousness or one falls from a state of uprightness. For that matter God is able to make one remain steadfast."

> *Him that is weak in the faith receive ye, but not to doubtful disputations. For one believeth that he may eat all things: another, who is weak, eateth herbs. Let not him that eateth despise him that eateth not; and let not him which eaterth not judge him that eateth: for God hath receicved him.*

> *Who art thou that judgest another man's servant? To his own master he standeth or falleth. Yea, he shall be holden up: for God is able to make him stand. One man esteemeth one day above another: another esteemeth every day alike. Let every man be fully persuaded in his own mind. He that regardeth the day regardeth it unto the Lord; and he that regardeth not the day, to the Lord he doth not regard it. He that eateth, eateth to the Lord, for he giveth God thanks: and he that eateth not, to the Lord he eateth not and giveth God thanks.*

> *For none of us liveth to himself and no man dieth to himself. For whether we live, we live unto the Lord; and whether we die, we die unto the Lord: whether we live therefore, or die, we are the Lord's. For to this end Christ both died and rose, and revived, that He might be Lord both of the dead and living.*

That is quite a rebuke yet for all it is worth they violate that principle.

I look at it this way. I go to a neighbour's home and with no regards for his code of conduct as directives given to his servants; I begin to order them around. Many of the things that I stipulate are contrary to the neighbours rules and regulations yet I insist that my instructions be executed. Regardless of how well intentioned I might have been, I have violated that neighbour. When it comes to God, it is infinitely worse. It is like walking into His heaven and proceeding to rearrange the furniture in His throne room. Who asked me to? With whose permission or authority do I do those things? Is God not wise enough to set things the way He wants them? Isn't it insulting to go in and rearrange things?

At my home, I run things the way I want to. If I leave a chair beside the door it is because I want it there. Who are you to walk in and say take it out of there that is not the place for it?

That is what God is saying to "day" keepers with relations to those He has called. You have no right to criticise whether he keeps a particular day or what he eats within bounds – no blood.

In I Corinthians 8:8 God repeats the same principle. He makes it plain that what we eat or do not eat does not make us any better or worse before Him. A greater principle governs our actions i.e. "what effect does it have on the weaker brother?" But lookout for those who would consider themselves "weaker" that through subtlety and deceit they bring you into bondage. To that end God commands in Colossians 2:16, "Do not allow, permit or suffer anyone to judge you in respect of meat, drink, and holidays or of the new moons or of the Sabbath days." In our St. Lucian context it means all the foods that some would forbid us from eating, celebrating holidays like Christmas and Easter seeking to follow the Jewish calendar; nor keeping the Saturday Sabbaths. All those who would seek to impose those upon you are infringing on your "liberty" and violating the command of God not to judge.

One needs to be very cautious with those who teach false doctrines. Those are not always easily detectable. But there are some indicators that we would do well to take heed of.

In I Timothy 4:1-6 we have a profile of those false teachers. One of the first things which characterises them is that they have departed from the faith. Their departure from the faith could either be simply teaching contrary to what God has said or a total leaving of a particular body of believers. Either way there is a departure from the faith.

Next, they listen to the voice of seducing spirits. These spirits sound genuine but their whole objective is to lead astray. Thus we need to be on our close guard against their influence.

Worse still, what they teach is from the devil. I told you that we are sometimes too tolerant. Some of the false teachings that seek to over run the church are from the pit of hell. Some of them are way out and are easily recognizable. There are others, though, that are not very apparent. They have a semblance of seeking God's righteousness but "denying the power thereof" (II Tim. 3:5).

Another trait is that they are evil men. Their mode of operation is to deceive for they themselves are deceived. The things they proclaim are meant to seduce thus may not sound too way out. The only antidote for those is to know the Scripture. Timothy was challenged to know the Scripture. We know the source of Biblical doctrine. Even the source of Biblical doctrine is seriously challenged today.

Paul gives us a list of things that mark the false teachers and teachings in Titus 3:9. These are foolish questions, genealogies, contentious striving about the Law. Yes striving about the Law is listed among those outstanding features. They are described as unprofitable. The passage goes on in verse 11 to describe them as subverted, is sinning and under self-inflicted condemnation.

You are no longer in the world, "therefore you are not controlled by the things of the world". Some of the restrictions that are being imposed upon us have to do only with the world. We must neither be brought under subjection of them nor by them (Gal. 4:9, 10; Col. 2:20-23). How much more can the Scriptures say to make us aware that our salvation is not in any way of our own making? Throughout scripture we are informed that we can do nothing to enhance or detract from our salvation. Salvation is by grace through faith. Grace, as we well know is unmerited favour. It is favour. We get it as a result of the goodwill of the one giving it. Grace is from God and not because we deserve it. The Bible specifically gives us an example of grace being attributed to Abraham. It was not his actions, though his actions demonstrated what his belief was. If the righteousness credited to him were as a result of any of his actions, then God would have been indebted to him and all that he had received would have been just payment. But all that Abraham received was as a result of the goodness of God so that it would be of grace and not of debt (Rom. 4).

Likewise, if my salvation depends on and comes as a result of my keeping the Sabbath day, I do have something to boast about. I would have to receive credit for having earned such benefit. But the Bible teaches us otherwise. Romans 6:23 calls it "the gift of God". It would be most foolish to have to work first and then settle for a gift in return for labour. It is either I have truly received a gift, which is totally unrelated to what I have done, or whatever was received was as a result of what I had done and therefore a just desert. No claim to having been given a gift could be justly made.

God does go on to specifically tell us that His gift of salvation is not because of any work that we have done (Tit. 3:5). Before God, all our righteousness is as filthy rags (Isa. 64:6). He continues the verse in Titus 3:5 by saying that His saving us is an act of mercy. Mercy is meted out when one has been an offender. We are all offenders and deserve condemnation and judgement. We could not save ourselves. "There is none righteous, no, not one" (Rom. 3:10). We are all under condemnation, unable to do anything about our condition (Rom. 3:23). Consequently, we had to have an outside source of help. God came to our aid with mercy. We have received something quite contrary to what we deserved. Keeping a Sabbath day does not enhance our standing in Christ.

Another deceitful trick used by the devil is to make the word 'commandments' in the New Testament refer only to the Old Testament Ten Commandments. In John 14:15 God says, *"If you love me keep my commandments"*. We would be made to believe that this reference is to the Decalogue. But the same John writing in I John 3:22, 23 simply states that we receive of God because we keep His commandments. What are His commandments – believe on the name of His Son, Jesus Christ; and love one another. That is not reference to the Decalogue yet these are commandments. We have commandments in all of the following passages for us as Christians to keep: I Tim. 4:1-6; II Tim 3:13ff; Titus 3:9; Gal. 4:9, 10; Col. 2:20ff. Numerous Laws are stated here and in the rest of the New Testament. Could there possibly be any connection between Christ's "keep my commandments" and those passages we have just mentioned.

One thing we should never forget, regardless of how much we argue or debate over the 'day', is that because of the inadequacy of the first covenant it was replaced with a second. Those are referred to as first and second despite the fact that there had been other covenants before the one referred to as 'first' and between the first and the one referred to as 'second'. The reason why those other covenants are not counted is because they were not for the same purpose of accomplishing righteousness in us as these two were (Rom. 10:4). The Ceremonial Law was not the standard or law being violated that required satisfaction but was the means of propitiating for the laws violated. The Laws violated that prevented the righteousness of its adherents were the Ten Commandments. Now Christ has become the propitiation for all of those violations that could not be adequately paid for by the sacrifices of animals and also for the sins of the present and future. Thank God for Jesus Christ.

But Christ being come an high priest of good things to come, by a greater and more perfect tabernacle, not made with hands, that is to say, not of this building; neither by the blood of goats and calves but by His own blood He entered in once into the holy place, having obtained **eternal redemption** *for us.*

For if the blood of bulls and of goats, and the ashes of an heifer sprinkling the unclean, sanctifieth to the purifying of the flesh: how much more shall the blood of Christ, who through the eternal Spirit offered himself without spot to God, purge your conscience from dead works to serve the living God?

*And for this cause He is the mediator of the New Testament, that by means of death, for the redemption of the transgressions that were under the first testament, they which are called might receive the promise **of eternal inheritance. (Heb. 9:11- 15)***

CHAPTER 10

CLOSING ADMONITION

No other passage of Scripture could adequately sum up the controversy of the Law versus Christian freedom as Galatians 5:1-4. This passage comes after much forceful arguments for the freedom of Christianity and against the prospect of re-enslavement in an unprofitable venture as keeping the Law.

In Galatians 5:1 Paul uses one of his favourite words because of the nature of the writing that he had just engaged in. In keeping with his usual forceful arguments for any cause that he presented or defended, he uses the word "therefore". As one former missionary pastor would say, "Anytime we come to this word, we need to ask ourselves the question, 'Wherefore is it therefore'?" The question is "why is he saying therefore"? As has been presented before Paul had been presenting his case in the contention that preceded his "therefore". Since an adequate case had been presented; since the arguments had been reasonable and logical and conclusive, he felt it most appropriate to draw the only correct, logical, fair, truthful conclusion.

"Therefore" does not stand in isolation. It has adequate support and under girding going before and also has the only possible conclusion coming after. He might well have said like the songwriter "I need no other argument I need no other plea".

"Therefore" sums it up in a way that leaves no room for other contention. Regardless of what other rationalization we may engage in, his conclusions under the direction of the Holy

Spirit puts the issue beyond the shadow of a doubt. To seek to add to or to conclude otherwise is to contravene the will and instruction of the Holy Spirit of God.

Paul's final word in the preceding chapter was to *'cast out the bond woman and her son; for the son of the bond woman shall not be heir with the son of the free woman.'* That was a very decisive final word and a foregone conclusion that proved the inappropriateness of paralleling the Law and Christianity. The two must never be considered as complimentary nor supplementary to each other for they are diametrically opposed. They are not in sync and therefore can never mesh.

Consequently, God had two very forceful imperatives for us following all the arguments against keeping Law. These were not suggestions that gave leeway for human choice but were definite commands that carried with them severe consequences. Failure to observe these commands, like every other command of God, carries penalties. To fail to keep these commandments is sin. Of course the wages of sin is death – but the gift of God is eternal life.

What are those commands of God given in His word through the Apostle Paul? We find the first command is to "**stand**". As with all imperatives where the subject is not stated we know it must be supplied; it is the person spoken to. The English language allows us the privilege of supplying "you". We can say then, "**You**, stand".

The command to stand requires of us that we assume a particular position. It commands us that we stand. To stand is to get up on our feet. It is not a relaxed or reclined position but one that requires much diligence and perseverance. It requires a firm connection to the object on which our feet are planted.

We live in a region where we are faced with the prospect of hurricanes for at least six months of the year. During the passage of a hurricane, we know that strong winds and much water batter the trees. These are two contriving forces that threaten the position of the tree. One undermines the foundation or root structure, loosening the soil around to render the tree vulnerable to the offensive power of the wind, which rocks the portion above ground in an effort to topple the tree.

Amazingly there are trees that will lose much of their branches because of the adverse conditions, but will remain steadfast despite all threats. Such a tree is well grounded. Our coconut tree is the most outstanding of the trees able to withstand. Although most often these trees are tall and top heavy yet they are so structured that they will bend into extremely threatening positions but as soon as the wind subsides will resume their original position.

God's command to us is to emulate the firmness and positive characteristics of such a tree. Not to be like one easily upended but one that will maintain its integrity as what it is.

But the command does not come without qualification. In this first command to stand we are told to, "**Stand fast**". We have recognized that adversities come to trees. We are no exceptions. Adversities such as were described in the preceding chapters seek to remove us from steadfastness in Christ to something that is otherwise. The command suggests that there is no other feasible place to move to. Whatever other location that one moves to is a place of certain destruction. The command is to 'stand fast' – be so firmly grounded that if the ground were to move, you would move with it. No transplant is necessary or possible.

Our stance is to be with great assurance and firmness. Adverse circumstances may threaten to move, uproot, to bend or to break us, but we are to remain steadfast in the doctrines that Christ taught and we have learned. To be persuaded otherwise is not an option. The command is to "stand fast".

Another qualifying phrase in the first command to "stand fast" is a description of the place where we are to be planted. Not all footing qualifies when we are to stand fast. There is a particular position; there is a particular place where nothing should move us. Some soils are more prone to move than others. Jesus Christ, Himself, made reference to those types of soil in the parable of the house on the rock. The house on the rock withstood the weather but the one on the plain soil fell flat (Mt.

7:24-29). The latter is typical of the type of response there is when one is unstable. Ephesians 4:14 continues to make us aware of the constant threat to our stability and also the antidote to counteract those onslaughts. Quite contrary to natural disasters we cannot always foretell the source and direction of our conflict, but we can always be prepared and always have the victory. We have been put on alert by Christ through the writers of scripture and have been commanded to be on our guard. Satan's attacks are not regular as seasons.

In this passage we are advised on where to stand fast. We should "**stand fast in the liberty**". Liberty here speaks of freedom to do or to omit things having no relations to salvation (Thayer's Greek/English Lexicon, pg. 204); I Cor. 10:29 – freedom from the yoke of the Mosaic Law – Gal.2:4; 5:1, 13; I Pet. 2:16; freedom from the dominion of corrupt desires so that we do by the free impulse of the soul what the will of God requires – II Cor.3:17.

Our freedom may be compared to a horse being released on a ranch that occupies hundreds of square miles. Two very obvious relationships may be drawn here. One is that the horse may never explore thoroughly the vastness of the spread at its disposal. Secondly, even in the areas that the horse explores it could be very selective. The same is true for the Christian. We can never comprehend the full extent of the freedom that God has made available to us. Yet in that which we occupy ourselves we have restrictions. Some of the restrictions are there because of our love for God; others because of conscience sake or for the sake of someone else. Self-imposed restrictions can change. It is also possible that though situations change we may choose not to revert to our former condition. These conditions are all matters of personal choice.

The command still remains – "*stand fast in the liberty…*" There is a quality to our *'liberty'*. It is not a liberty that has been acquired in rebellion against the status quo. Nor is it a freedom regardless of who likes or does not like it. It did not come as a result of a coup against all authority. But it came as a result of the Final Authority, Christ, releasing us to serve Him. This service comes not because we are on a long leash but because we are unfettered. It comes not because of such favours as Satan accused God of in the case of Job, but as a result of the love God demonstrated to us. The only natural and correct response to such love is to return love. As we return love, we need not slave over it but in all freedom allow it to flow. We love Him because He first loved us (I Jn. 4:7-11).

Beloved, let us love one another: for love is of God: and every one that loveth is born of God, and knoweth God. He that loveth not knoweth not God; for God is love. In this was manifested the love of God toward us, because that God sent His only begotten Son into the world, that we might live through him. Herein is love, not that we loved God, but that He loved us, and sent His Son to be the propitiation for our sins. Beloved, if God so loved us, we ought also to love one another.

Christians today are not living in rebellion against God and seeking to change laws in fulfilment of prophecies in Daniel 7:25. *If the Son therefore shall make you free, you shall be free indeed* (Jn. 8:36). Christ has freed us from the bondage of the Law having met all the requirements of its just demands. We are further called upon to be dead to the Law so that we may be married to Christ. This new relationship with Christ cannot be possible unless there is first the dying to the Law. One who is holding on to the Law and at the same time desiring that marriage relationship with Christ is seeking to foster an adulterous relationship with Him of which He, Christ, will have no part (Rom 7:1-4).

So the first command to us in resolution of the Christian freedom versus Law controversy is to "**stand fast in the liberty wherewith Christ hath made us free**".

The second command is similar, but it is forbidding.

It would be very disheartening to see an animal, which loves freedom, fettered; and because of obstacles, tangled to the extent that it can hardly move. You in your mercy and kind-heartedness took it upon yourself to release that animal. Not only did you untangle it but also you removed the obstacles that caused it to tangle. You further cut the animal loose so that it has unfettered freedom. No rope to restrict the extent of its movement. But, alas! The animal will not move from the spot where it was imprisoned. Despite your coaxing and prodding the animal seems to remain fettered, bound to the place where it had lost its freedom. As hopeless as the situation may seem, this is exactly what those who would have us under the Law are doing.

God commands us – "**Be not entangled…**" We seem to be understanding creatures of God, unlike the animal kingdom. We move, not by instinct as animals do but by the exercise of a will and choice. In making our decisions, we are commanded. That is a very powerful motivator to follow directions. Yet, we are left at liberty to go against those instructions as we see clearly demonstrated today.

The problem is that we were once in that predicament. We were helpless were it not for the grace of God. Now that we have been set free, we are cautioned – "**Be not entangled again…**"

That word 'again' carries with it implications that sound ominous. There seems to be the sound of a threat but whether such is disastrous – God knows. But to go contrary to God's command is most definitely sinful.

"Again" says that you were once there. Considering the fact that you were once there and that the conditions were repressive (against us); it further implies that you are not there any more. You have been removed from the oppressive situation. But it also suggests that you could return to that same master. It further suggests that if you choose to return, you will not be prevented. Finally, it suggests that whatever happens when you return would be consequential and your fault. Thus the command carries with it a plea.

"Be not entangled again with the yoke."

A yoke is a burden placed on the necks of animals so that they could be further burdened with backbreaking work. Many animals cringe under the burden especially when they are new to work. This yoke is not one that is amicable. God calls it "bondage".

As we consider the New Testament we see that three out of the eight times 'yoke' is mentioned it is in the negative. In Acts 15:10 it is a temptation or provocation to God. In Gal 5:1 it is bondage. Once we are warned against being unequally yoked together with unbelievers (II Cor. 6:14). Once a man used the excuse that he had bought six yoke of oxen to stay out of fellowship with God (Lk. 14:19). On one occasion, servants, who had become Christians, were admonished to consider their masters of more honour (I Tim. 6:1). Once, Paul refers to co-workers as 'true yokefellows'. And only twice were we invited to carry a yoke – Christ's yoke (Mt. 11:29, 30). Of course we don't wear literal yokes, but the analogy is very real. We become bogged down with the burdens that we place on ourselves, not to mention the fact that we are living in disobedience to God.

But the worst of it is that our yoke is one of slavery. Self inflicted or willingly enslaved. In the natural, we have all kinds of horrid stories of slavery – from the slave trade, the middle passage, the fields and even the torment of persons who were and still want to be slave owners and masters. We hate even persons that have that kind of mentality. Yet in the spirit realm we place ourselves or allow ourselves to be put under slavery. God has freed us from servitude – whether to sin or to keeping Law. We have been liberated. Why seek again to be placed under such "bondage"?

Jesus Christ encountered those who would have others under that yoke of bondage. He said of them that they were wicked oppressors. What they would not attempt to touch with a finger is what they impose on others. On another occasion, Jesus Christ had to admonish that we should not muzzle the ox that treads out the corn. There is strong suggestion in this command that the forces that be were repressive and cruel. They will not allow a moment's pleasure or even 'refuelling' while they drain the lifeblood out of you.

Later In the book of Galatians, we are informed that this action is not of God. This information is an eye opener while at the same time very scary (Gal. 5:8). The Scriptures tell us that God has called us out of darkness into His marvellous light.

> *But you are a chosen generation, a royal priesthood, an holy nation, a peculiar people; that you should show forth the praises of him who have called you out of darkness into His marvellous light:* (1 Pet. 2:9)

We are also cautioned that the devil transforms Himself into an angel of light and so do his agents (II Cor. 11:13-15).

> *For such are false apostles, deceitful workers, transforming themselves into the apostles of Christ. And no marvel; for Satan himself is transformed into an angel of light. Therefore it is no great thing if his ministers also be transformed as the ministers of righteousness; whose end shall be according to their works*

The thing is that whatever the devil presents may very well look like something that God Himself might present. Great Spiritual discernment is necessary to differentiate between the two.

But we have a head start in knowing what we are getting into when we seek to be enslaved again. God tells us also, *"This persuasion cometh not of Him who calleth you"*. It begs the question, then, 'who is behind that persuasion?' If not from God, then from whom? There is only one logical answer to this question. If it is not God, it must be the devil.

Many of us go sentimental and emotional about it right at this point. We know too many "good people" who hold that view and propagate the poison who seem so harmless and friendly. They sometimes demonstrate better Christian lives than some others who do not hold unto their view and name the name of Christ. These arguments are all satanic subtleties. We well know that you catch more flies with syrup than with vinegar. What the devil presents is seldom repulsive for he knows that god-fearing persons will not bite. It resembles the truth enough to make it acceptable to the unsuspecting. We would do well to remember that this persuasion is not of Him who calls you.

As difficult as the truth might be we must realize that our human rationalizations are not what count in the final analysis. God has made a declaration that to go that way is not of Him.

More terrifying statements are used of that way as we look at the scriptures. In Galatians 5:4 we are informed that to accept the law removes us from the realm of depending on the substitutionary work of Christ to justification by works. *"Christ has become of no effect unto you."* You cannot claim justification by grace through faith in Christ Jesus while you labour to satisfy God through your own efforts. Anything you may attain will have to be reckoned as a debt and not of grace through faith. The Law is not of faith. There are no two ways about it (Gal. 3:11, 12).

> But that no man is justified by the law in the sight of God, it is evident: for, the just shall live by faith. And the law is not of faith: but, the man that doeth them shall live in them.

Another horrific situation stares one in the face when one seeks to establish again the bondage of the Law. Galatians 5:4 says, *"You are fallen from grace."* Two scenarios immediately come to mind as I contemplate this possibility. The one is that a person though not yet saved, might have been on a level where grace was available. But to embrace self-effort as opposed to the grace of God is to remove one from the level of possibility and availability to one of impossibility. As long as one depends on his own efforts for salvation, justification will continue to elude him. The other scenario is of one who once believed but has turned from faith in

God to faith in ones own efforts. A horror stricken image of Peter readily comes to mind. As long as his gaze was fixed on Jesus, he walked on the water. As soon as his eyes shifted from Christ to his circumstances or efforts, he began to sink. He fell to another level. He started well, help was within reach but he was sinking. He had to turn again to Jesus Christ's salvation.

How much that resembles many who have started in Christ but have fallen to the place where they seek completion in the works of the Law. Satan had come along with the well-known story, i.e. "You have taken a good step. One thing you lack though is that you must keep the commandments". The gullible fall for it. They are still 'children tossed to and fro by every wind of doctrine'. How many times we have heard the statement – "now I've found the truth". My retort is if you did not know before that what you had was not the truth, how are you assured now that what you have is the truth? Satan is a wicked deceiver.

Still another statement looms before us that I even cringe when I say it. But God's word tells us in Revelation 2:9 *"I know the blasphemy of them which say they are Jews and are not, but are the synagogue of Satan"*. We have among us those who claim to be Jews, albeit spiritual Jews, and are not. The Church of Jesus Christ is comprised of people of every race and tongue but is not characterised by a particular nationality. In the Church of God we cease to retain racial difference but have attained an oneness in Christ that is unique. We are neither Jews nor gentiles not bound nor free, not even male nor female; but we are one. We share the same title and we share the same shed blood (Gal. 3:28). To claim a Jewish identity especially when you are not a Jew by natural descent is to place yourself in the category that Jesus Christ just described here. 'It is blasphemy', He says. I don't know, but if God says it is so, it must be so. All care should be taken. If God says that such saying is blasphemy and you say that you have not blasphemed, you face the further charge of calling God a liar. That is double jeopardy. God goes on to further clarify who those so-called Jews are. They are members of the synagogue or church of Satan. What a terrible tag to be carrying. Many around you may not recognize you, either because of friendship or through ignorance but there is no hiding away from God. I would, in no way, want to be identified as a member of the church of Satan.

Those who advocate the Law would claim in their defence that they believe in salvation by grace through faith. They lie. If when a person does not keep the Law, especially the Sabbath, he is not saved, then His salvation is dependant on his adherence to the Law. Titus 3:5 says it is *"not by works of righteousness which we have done, but according to His mercy He saved us."* Herein lies the deception of Satan to those who would believe in the Law. He will not allow you to believe outright in Christ. We must be dead to the Law in order to be married to Christ. No spiritual adultery.

Why run the risk of being rejected by God for trying to attain His favour by keeping a set of laws that you do not need to keep in order to have you on His side? It is foolhardy. It is better to throw yourself on the mercies of God, rest in His promises and be assured of your eternal hope than to try in your own strength knowing from the outset that you are doomed to failure. Those who had the Law never kept it (Gal. 6:13; Jer. 31:32).

For neither they themselves who are circumcised keep the law; but desire to have you circumcised, that they may glory in your flesh.

Not according to the covenant that I made with their fathers in the day that I took them by the hand to bring them out of the land of Egypt; which my covenant they brake, although I was an husband unto them, saith the LORD.

We repeat the clarion call to all believers, "**stand fast in the liberty wherewith Christ hath made you free and be not entangled again with the yoke of bondage**" (Gal. 5:1). Christians, we are not ignorant of Satan's devises. We are not ignorant of his activities in the world around us today in the persons of those who would enslave us again. We have been fore warned. We have been cautioned. There is no reason to fall prey to the devises of the devil.

The Sabbath served its time and purpose. But today we serve a risen Saviour. We serve a Christ who by example initiated Sunday as the day to worship Him. Even then He does not hold a big stick over our heads to force conformity to a day but still allows that with our newfound liberty, we can use every day and any day (Rom. 14:5, 6).

BIBLIOGRAPHY

Thompson, F.C. *The New Chain Reference Bible*; 58th. Printing; B.B. Kirkbridge Bible Co Inc.,

Scofield, Rev. C. I., D. D. *The Scofield Study Bible*; Oxford University Press, Inc.

Dake, Fanis Jennings; *Dakes Annotated Reference Bible*; Dake Bible Sales, Inc. P.O. Box 1050, Lawrenceville, Georgia 30246

Strong, James: *Strong's Exhaustive Concordance*; Associated Publishers and Authors Inc., Grand Rapids, Michigan 49315

Thayer, Joseph Henry D.D. PhD.; *Thayer's Greek-English Lexicon of the New Testament;* Associated Publishers and Authors, Inc. Grand Rapids, Michigan 49315

Dictionaries: *Longman's Dictionary of Contemporary English*: Pitman Press; ELBS 1979

Webster's New World Dictionary of the American Language: The World Publishing co. New York and Cleveland; ↑ 1970

www.ingramcontent.com/pod-product-compliance
Lightning Source LLC
Chambersburg PA
CBHW031225120626
46545CB00003B/991